DUNG

DUNG

A festering pile of fantastic facts
and gross animal antics

WARNING!

And we do mean REALLY gross.
Don't say we didn't warn you!

text by Michael Powell
illustrations by David Mostyn

Robinson Children's Books

First published in the UK by Robinson Children's Books
an imprint of Constable & Robinson, 2001

Constable & Robinson Ltd
3 The Lanchesters
162 Fulham Palace Road
London W6 9ER
www.constablerobinson.com

Text © Michael Powell
Illustration © David Mostyn

A copy of the British Library Cataloguing in Publication Data for
this title is available from the British Library.

ISBN 1 84119 355 0

10 9 8 7 6 5 4 3 2 1

CONTENTS

INTRODUCTION

Welcome to DUNG — a festering pile of fantastic facts and gross animal antics. If you're looking for cute stuff, forget it. Inside DUNG, you'll meet all kinds of animals from peeing pets and barfing birds to farting sharks and poop-loving killer ants. Remember — if it isn't gross, it isn't here!

Want to find out why dogs drag their bums along the floor, why bushbabies pee on their hands or how big was the biggest dinosaur poo? Look no further. You'll find all the answers in DUNG. And along the way, you'll meet a crowd of colourful creatures, including the chicken that survived for four years WITHOUT A HEAD, animals that eat their own parents, and sheep that can shear themselves. There's even a top 20 of animal killers and an A–Z of animal parasites. (You'll freak out when you discover just how many live in YOUR BEDROOM!)

AND if you dare, try the quiz on page 202 to discover just how gross YOU are. There's no escape . . . remember, we're all animals, too!

So go on! Dive into this fresh and steaming glob of gruesome animal grossology.

You have been warned . . .

Michael Powell

CHAPTER ONE
CHOW DOWN!

Animals eat weird things, and many catch their prey in unusual ways. Some animals eat ENORMOUS amounts; others survive for weeks without food. But however often they chow down, most animals have their fair share of disgusting eating habits, ranging from chomping their poop to eating their own legs.

So, what are you waiting for? Press your nose against this restaurant window of animal life and read on . . . just don't expect to have an appetite afterwards. This little lot will REALLY put you off your food!

INCY WINCY SPIDERS

Let's start with the Portia — a spider that eats other spiders.

The Portia lands on another spider's web and gives it a quick shake. The web spider creeps out thinking it has caught a juicy, wriggling bug. Instead, it runs into the Portia and realizes, all too late, that IT'S the one on the menu . . .

Animal cannibal
Another spider is even grosser. The black widow spider is a real cannibal. The female eats her partner after mating and can gobble up as many as 25 mates in a single day. Yeuuch!

Perhaps the grossest spiders of all are baby crab spiders observed by Australian scientists. These spiders bite off their mother's limbs and feed on them for several weeks!

Webs for tea?
Spiders aren't fussy eaters and some have been known to gobble up their own webs when they are thirsty. Webs absorb water so, if water is scarce, a spider can survive by simply eating itself out of house and home.

Spiders in a spin

Scientists love spiders because they are so freakish. In the 1960s, animal researchers fed a group of spiders with flies that they had injected with caffeine. The spiders got extremely fidgety and spun some very wacky webs (and probably stayed up all night). When the researchers fed their spiders sedatives, the spiders simply fell asleep.

Very fishy...

There is even a large spider that enjoys fishing for its prey. The fishing spider sticks its leg into the water and waggles it around very fast. When a curious tadpole or small fish comes over to peer at the disturbance, the spider sticks its head under the water, grabs the fish with its powerful jaws and drags it to the surface to eat.

MAD MYTH

Q: Does the average person REALLY swallow around ten spiders a year while they're asleep?

A: Have you heard this one, too? Well, you'll be pleased to know that although you might be a big sucker, you've probably never swallowed a spider in your sleep yet. Think about it. What do you do when you sleep? You breathe (hopefully). And what do spiders avoid? Predators. And since all the animals that like eating spiders also breathe, it would have to be a very dumb spider to walk into an open breathing mouth.

Yes, you say, but what if it accidentally falls from the ceiling into my mouth? Well, how big is your ceiling? Quite large probably. And how big is your mouth? Ideally, much smaller than your ceiling. So there is only a minuscule chance that an eight-legged creature is going to accidentally perform a rope-less bungee jump straight into your mouth. You've got more chance of innocently snacking on a Guatemalan dorito frog. And if you really believe there is such a thing then there's no hope for you. You'd better sleep with your mouth shut.

TELL ME WHY

BELLYACHE

Spiders aren't the only animals that have strange feeding habits. The gastric brooding frog was discovered in Australia in 1972 but, sadly, is now extinct. The mother raised her brood of about 30 tadpoles in a very unusual way. She would fast for eight weeks and switch off her digestive juices to allow her babies to develop inside her stomach. When the tadpoles outgrew her expanding belly, she would open her mouth wide and burp up a ready-made family.

Killer babies
You might consider that renting out your stomach to your children is very laid-back parenting, but what about an insect called the cecidomyian gall midge?

In certain conditions, this midge is partheno-genetic, which means that it can produce young on its own, without needing a mate. Parthenogenesis is amazing enough, but what happens next is awesome.

The babies (maggots) develop within the mother's tissues, eventually taking over her whole body. Then, as they grow, they eat her up from the inside and finally burst out of her body a few days later, leaving just a shell. Within two days those killer babies will begin the whole process again, as their own children begin to eat THEM up from within.

Q: Which animal gets lunch with its bum?

A: An African mongoose has a bottom that looks like a little flower (sweet!). It sits in a bush with its bum in the air and waits for an unsuspecting insect to arrive. Then, just as the insect is having a good sniff, the mongoose eats it up! (It probably does the poor insect a favour. I mean, imagine having to admit to your mates that you've just sniffed a mongoose's bum. "It looked just like a flower, honest!" Of course it did . . .)

TELL ME WHY

GREEDY BUG

Have you ever heard of the eating habits of the female praying mantis? During mating, the smaller male jumps on the back of the larger female. If he mistimes the jump, he ends up getting eaten. Even if he's successful and begins mating, the female will often rotate her head 180 degrees and bite his head off! The headless male is still capable of mating, after which the female eats the rest of him. Now there's a real case of the munchies . . .

MAD MYTH

Eating the roasted eggs of a praying mantis is a cure for bed-wetting.

BIG BUG

The bug with the biggest appetite has to be the larva of the polypemus moth, which can be found chowing down in North America. During the first two days of its life it eats 86,000 times its own body weight. That's the same as a 3.2kg (7lb) baby eating 269 tonnes (tons) or 1.5 million jars of baby food.

Heavy rockers

One thing is for certain. Insects have BIG appetites. A swarm of locusts can eat 80,000 tonnes (tons) of corn in a single day. And according to a recent scientific study, when termites are played hard rock music, it makes them even more hungry and they eat their way through wood at twice their normal speed!

Q: Why are some animals cannibals?

A: There are two types of animal cannibal. The "passive" ones (such as crabs and crows) do not hunt and kill their own kind, but they will eat the sick or dead. "Active" cannibals, on the other hand (like alligators), deliberately hunt their own kind. This behaviour does have its advantages. When food is scarce, it is better that some creatures survive by eating the weaker ones rather than they all die.

Even peaceful animals, such as mice, can turn cannibal if they are subjected to very harsh conditions, such as severe overcrowding. Some animals (like lions) kill the young of their rivals to make sure that their own offspring are favoured.

Then there are poor old ladybird larvae, which simply eat each other by mistake . . . Aaah!

MAD MYTH

To protect yourself from bubonic plague, wear a spider in a walnut shell around your neck.

JOKE CORNER

How do you stop a cockerel crowing on Sunday morning?
Have him for dinner on Saturday night.

What do you get if you run over a bird with a lawn-mower?
Shredded tweet.

What did the girl maggot say to the boy maggot?
"What's a nice girl like you doing in a joint like this?"

What did the skunk say when the wind changed direction?
"Ah, it's all coming back to me now."

Why did the hedgehog cross the road?
To see his flat mate.

A little verse . . .
Little pigeon in the sky,
Dropping things from way up high.
Farmer George wipes his eye,
"Oh, thank goodness cows can't fly!"

POOPER SCOOPERS

There are lots of mammals with unusual appetites and eating habits, too. For example, did you know that a rabbit digests its food twice? How? By eating its own poop, of course. This means that its body gets to soak up all the nutrients that it didn't catch the first time round and it helps to give its stomach a high bacterial count. (By the way, rabbits also love eating liquorice . . .)

Baby elephants also eat poop. When they're little, they eat their mother's dung because it contains tiny organisms to help them digest their food. They don't tell you that in *Dumbo*, do they?

TELL ME WHY

Q: Which insect drinks buffalo tears?

A: Moths love to swarm around the heads of buffalo and feed on their tears. But they don't have to waste time looking for a sad, weepy one. They settle on a buffalo's eyelid, jab the poor buffalo repeatedly in the eye with their proboscis to make it cry, then lap up the tears.

TELL ME WHY

ANOTHER BANANA, DEER?

What do you think are the two things that reindeer can't get enough of (apart from dragging Santa's luggage through the sky, once a year)? Give up? Bananas and moss, of course! They love moss, not because it's any good for them, but because it contains a special chemical that acts like antifreeze and stops them turning into snowdeer (get it?).

WHAT A CATCH!

Many fish are great fishers themselves and some have developed unusual ways of catching their prey.

Going fishing . . .
Some species of angler fish, found off the coasts of Europe and North Africa, have fishing rods sticking out of the top of their heads. Some even have fake worms on the end of their rods. When other fish come up to investigate or munch on the worms, the angler fish snaps them up.

Shallow-water angler fish can grow up to 2m (6ft) long and 40kg (88lb) in weight. They have huge mouths so they can swallow fish as big as themselves. Conger eels, crabs, dogfish and even seabirds have been found in their stomachs.

Angler fish are also extremely greedy. After they have eaten, their stomach contents make up one-third of their entire body weight. In fact, these angler fish are the real couch potatoes of the fish world. They lie motionless on the seabed for long periods, so they don't need powerful swimming muscles or large gills like other fish. This means that the rear part of their bodies is very underdeveloped, making them little more than big gobs with fins!

MORE FISHY STORIES

Angler fish don't win all the prizes for gross behaviour and strange ways of getting their lunch. Take a look at these fishy friends.

Light lures
There is a group of deep-sea fish that use lights to attract a meal. The viper fish is one of these, with an amazing 1,350 fairy lights in its mouth. The bottom of the ocean floor is a very grim and boring place, so any fish that can pretend to be a nightclub is bound to be a winner!

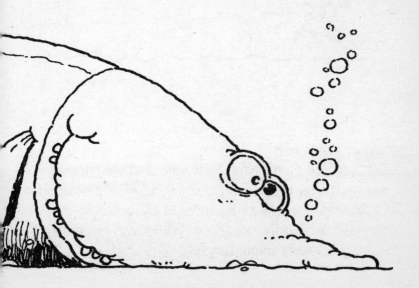

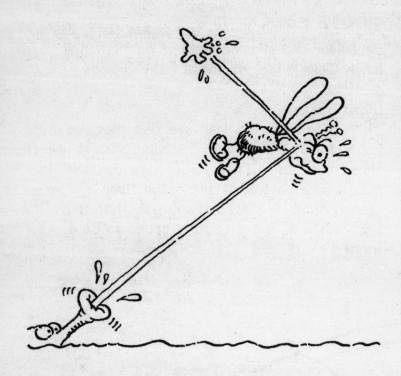

Super spitter
The archer fish from Australia and Southeast
Asia puts on a dazzling display of marksmanship.
It knocks down passing insects by gobbing at
them with deadly accuracy. (Whoever named it
missed a great opportunity!)

Big gob

But you don't need gimmicks to catch fish if you've got a huge mouth. Gulper fish don't go in for any flash stuff. They just swim around with their huge mouths gaping wide open. OK, it's not subtle, but it works!

Snap happy

The alligator-snapping turtle uses a similar "lying-motionless-with-mouth-open" technique to find food. It is so inactive that small plants grow on its shell, helping to camouflage it. A big pink dangly thing at the back of its mouth is irresistible to curious fish, who wander by and poke their heads into the turtle's mouth to get a better look. The turtle then snaps its jaws shut and it's curtains for the fish.

Skin care

In some places, fish literally line up to be eaten alive, or rather, licked clean. Along the reefs of the Indian Ocean, fish of all shapes and sizes queue up at special skin-cleaning stations, where armies of busy cleaning shrimps gobble up dead scraps of skin and little parasites, leaving their satisfied customers with a healthy complexion. Without this invaluable twice-daily grooming, the fish would soon become infested with parasites and get seriously ill.

MAD MYTH

It is unlucky to say the words "dog" and "pig" when at sea.

PIG!

TELL ME WHY

Q: Which animal eats its own arms when it gets stressed?

A: When under severe stress, some octopuses will eat their own tentacles. Hey, when you're feeling nervous and you've got eight arms, why not have a snack? What's really cool is that they grow back later anyway. So you can be sure that when an octopus invites a few friends around to watch a scary movie, there's still plenty to eat when the pizza runs out!

TELL ME WHY

SLOPPY SECONDS

With all this talk of eating, we mustn't forget those animals that make barfing a big part of their lives. The housefly, for instance, is a top puker. It just loves to throw up on its food and then eat it. The puke actually helps to digest the food before it's swallowed.

Everyone knows that dogs like to eat grass to help them to retch. Or do they? Well, it's not really true. Dogs don't need anything to help them vomit, they're just so good at it! Their cousins, wolves, can eat their dinner and then travel long distances before regurgitating it to feed to their pups.

Many snakes sick up the bones of the other animals that they eat. They don't chew; they swallow things whole. Some can even dislocate their jaws to swallow really big animals!

And birds just love to barf, too. For example, after an owl has eaten, say, a mouse, it produces a furry pellet containing the mouse's skeleton.

TELL ME WHY

Q: What is the polite way to be sick if you are a frog?

A: The polite way to be sick in froggy society is first, hurl so powerfully that your stomach pops out of your mouth and is left dangling. Second, scrape out the puke with your forearms and, third, swallow your stomach.

TELL ME WHY

YOU MAKE ME SICK!

The frigate bird must have a cruel sense of humour because it doesn't throw up itself. Instead, it chases after other birds and makes THEM sick up their lunch. Then it tucks into the sloppy seconds. Yuck! And all this takes place in midair! The frigate bird will also eat the young of other birds whenever it gets the chance.

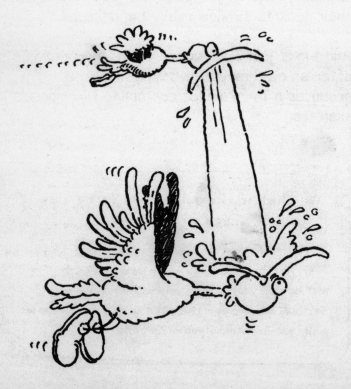

Q: Is honey really just bee puke?

A: Worker bees collect nectar from flowers and keep it in a special stomach (separate from their other stomach) where chemicals begin to break it down and turn it into honey. The worker bee returns to the nest where it pukes up the honey, fans it with its wings to help remove excess moisture, shoves it into a honeycomb, then seals it up with wax. So, yes, that's the stuff that ends up on your breakfast table — bee puke (well, kind of). Now they don't tell you that on the jar!

HALL OF FAME

The North American turkey vulture

The turkey vulture has to be one of the most disgusting birds in the world. Not only does it enjoy feasting on decaying flesh, but it is also a top barfer. Never mess with a turkey vulture because when it feels threatened it will vomit a disgusting mixture of partially digested rotting meat over an intruder. This not only freaks out the attacker but makes the bird lighter so that it can fly away more easily.

The turkey vulture's scientific name is *Cathartes aura* (pronounced kath-are-teez ow-rah), meaning "purifying vulture". Presumably this is a reference to its puking ability and does not mean it's a clean-living kind of creature.

The word "vulture" comes from the Latin word *vulturus* meaning "tearer" — a reference to how it rips up its food. Turkey vultures are about 75cm (30in) long and weigh just under 2kg (around 3–4lb). They have small red heads and dark brown bodies and look a lot like turkeys.

Unlike most birds, turkey vultures have a very powerful sense of smell, which means they can detect carrion (dead stuff) very easily. (Sad, really. If you've got to eat rotting flesh, you don't want to have to smell it too!) In fact, they have even been used in the gas industry to detect leaks. Natural gas has no smell, so gas companies add chemicals to give it one. And one of the chemicals, called ethyl mercaptan, is also given off by rotting flesh. So that's why if you see turkey vultures circling overhead, it may be the sign of a gas leak below. Remember the next time you smell gas, you're also experiencing the smell of rotting flesh!

As if they weren't gross enough, when turkey vultures want to cool down, instead of reaching for a drink, they excrete down their legs. The scientific name for this is "thermoregulation" (meaning heat control) — call it what you like; I say the turkey vulture dumps on its own feet.

FUSSY FEEDER

So, you see, animals are a gross and faddy bunch when it comes to eating. But the award for the fussiest eater of them all has to go to the flamingo, which can only eat when its head is upside down! There's a good reason for this. It feeds by standing in water and swinging its head back and forth. In this way, lots of water passes through its bill, which acts like a special filter, trapping any food, such as small molluscs and insect larvae.

Flamingos also have thick and powerful tongues which help them to pump water through their bills. Along with parrotfish livers, peacock brains and lamprey guts, flamingo tongues were considered top nosh among decadent Roman emperors around 2,000 years ago!

Q: Why don't scavengers get food poisoning?

A: Animals do get food poisoning and some of them die as a result. However, some people argue that scavenging animals have developed a greater resistance to the microbes and poisons in their food. And yet no animals go out of their way to eat things that are likely to cause them harm. For example, most animals will avoid eating the manure of other animals from the same species. However, as we have already discovered, some animals do enjoy eating poop.

Contrary to what you might expect, rats are particularly cautious. If they ever eat something that makes them ill they will never eat it again. Dogs and wolves, on the other hand, eat whatever they fancy and just sick up anything that disagrees with them. Apparently coyotes are so skilled at vomiting that poisoning them is a skill in itself.

Other people argue that most bacteria from decomposing carcasses are not toxic or disease-making, and stomach acids can kill most bacteria. Humans eat some really weird stuff and they don't get sick either. For example, a Scandinavian delicacy is rotting fish. And pheasant-lovers believe that it tastes better after it has been well "hung", or left in the open air and allowed to decompose for a while. After all, when you think about it, cheese and yoghurt are just rotten milk.

TOP FOOD FACTS

- It takes 40 minutes to hard-boil an ostrich egg.

- A shrew eats its own weight in food every three hours or so.

- A giraffe can last longer without water than a camel.

- A cow gives nearly 200,000 glasses of milk in her lifetime.

- A camel's milk does not curdle.

- A sheep will not drink from running water.

- A carnivorous animal will not eat another animal if it has been struck by lightning.

- A young robin eats about 4m (13ft) of earthworms every day.

- Hippo milk is bright pink.

- A crocodile has so much acid in its stomach it could digest steel.

- If a hummingbird doesn't eat at least every 30 minutes when awake, it will starve to death.

- A snake can eat an animal four times larger than the width of its head.

- Penguins can turn salty water into drinking water through a hole in their foreheads.

- The duckbill platypus of Australia can keep more than 600 worms in its cheek pouches.

- To survive, birds need to eat at least half their own weight in food every day.

- Toads eat only moving prey.

Yes, animals do love their food — whatever it is. So, next time you eat, just think of what you could be tucking into right now if you weren't human. But what happens when animals tuck into US? Turn the page to discover a whole heap of gross and scary ANIMAL KILLERS . . .

CHAPTER TWO
ANIMAL KILLERS

We've already seen that animals have some freaky feeding habits, but what happens when WE are on the menu?

Here is the **DUNG Top 20** most dangerous
animals to humans — hand-picked for their
ability to crush, bite, rip, poison, maim and tear
us limb from limb. Some are highly poisonous
while others just have enormous teeth and a
seriously bad attitude . . .

« 20 »
MAN-EATING LION

The lion is the second-largest of the big cats —
only the tiger is bigger. You don't want to mess
with ANY of the big cats, which include the
cheetah, leopard and jaguar, but while they are
all pretty scary, perhaps the scariest of all is
the idea of a man-eating (and woman-eating!)
lion.

In India and Africa at the end of the nineteenth century, legends grew up in certain areas
where man-eating lions kept attacking people.

There is a famous case of two enormous man-eaters that attacked more than 130 workers who were building a bridge over the Tsavo River in Kenya during a nine-month reign of terror. When they were eventually shot and their skulls were examined, it was discovered that one of the animals had a broken tooth and a large abscess, so most likely it was only hunting humans out of desperation.

Lions use their powerful canine teeth to grab the throat or sever the spinal column of large prey such as a zebra or buffalo, but a lion with an abscess would be unable to kill in this way. Animals can be at their most dangerous when they are sick or wounded.

‹‹ 19 ››
KILLER BEE

In the film *The Swarm*, thousands of people were stung to death by swarms of killer bees, but do killer bees really exist? Well, there *is* a very aggressive and unpleasant bee that is rapidly spreading through the United States called the "Africanized bee". It was created in the 1950s when Brazilian scientists cross-bred bees in an attempt to improve honey production.

Unfortunately, what they ended up with was a vicious, aggressive bee that didn't produce much honey!

Like other bees, Africanized bees swarm when they are threatened. The difference with this monster, however, is that it can stay angry for days. All it takes is for one bee to sting. This releases a chemical alarm that arouses all the other bees. Then, off they go, looking for a fight. The bees will chase a moving target for up to 400m (1,300ft). Fortunately, though, they are slow fliers, so most healthy humans can outrun them.

≪ 18 ≫
SCORPION

This eight-legged stinger is a close relative of the spider but it famously packs a sting in its tail. There are around 1,300 species of scorpion worldwide and they don't all live in the desert. Scorpions have even been found in the Himalayas and Andes mountains.

There are only about 20 species of scorpion that are really harmful to humans, but who's taking any chances? Especially when the little stingers can track you down with up to six pairs of eyes!

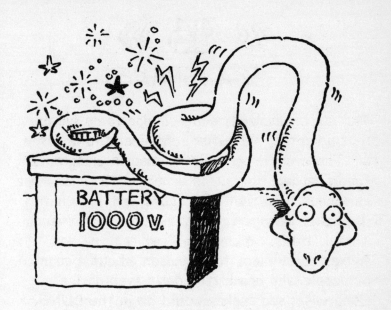

‹‹ 17 ››
ELECTRIC EEL

An eel is actually a kind of fish that can grow up to 2m (6ft) long and weigh more than 23kg (50lb). Electric eels can really pack a punch when fully charged – just one of these stunners can give off up to 1,000 volts of electricity, which is enough to knock out a human! When they have eaten their stunned prey, the eels go and hide under a rock while they recharge, ready for their next victim.

‹‹ 16 ››
SEA SNAKE

The sea snake looks quite similar to an eel, but it is a reptile, not a fish, and needs to breathe air. However, it can hold its breath underwater for up to two hours. Its venom is 10 times more poisonous than that of a cobra, but fortunately it doesn't manage to deliver much of the venom when it bites. So amazingly, while some sea snakes carry mega-toxic poison, about a quarter of people who are bitten don't even notice. Otherwise, sea snakes would be in the **DUNG Top 10** animal killers.

‹‹ 15 ››
SHARK

Sharks have been around for more than 400 million years and haven't changed much in the last 100 million years or so. There are about 400 different species of shark and most of them — about 80 per cent — are harmless to humans. For example, one species of shark is so tiny, it's fully grown when it is just 15cm (6in) long.

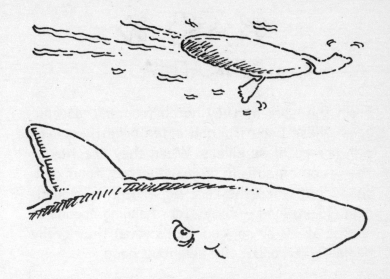

Every year, there are between 50 and 75 attacks on humans by sharks. Of this number, only around 10 attacks are fatal — that's less than the number of people killed by elephants, bees, crocodiles and even donkeys! However, the great white, the tiger and the bull shark do have fearsome reputations, even though many of their attacks on humans may well be a case of mistaken identity — from under the water, someone on a surfboard looks very much like a seal.

Most sharks circle and poke their prey before attacking, but the great white is most feared not only because of the success of the film *Jaws*, but because it is the only shark that relies upon surprise and will attack without warning.

«« 14 »»
PIRANHA

From the moment they hatch from microscopic eggs, these beautiful and often brightly coloured fish are ruthless killers. When they are tiny, they feed on cute little crustaceans, fruit and seeds, but when they are big enough — around 4cm (1⅝in) long — they start hanging around in posses of 20 or so, and that's when they really begin to terrorize the neighbourhood.

Piranha don't kill their prey before eating it. Instead, they eat it alive, stripping off its flesh with their razor-sharp teeth in a matter of minutes. They have even been known to grab drinking cattle and drag them into the water by their noses.

«« 13 »»
BLACK WIDOW SPIDER

It is the female black widow spider that is highly venomous. The male is half the size of the female and is completely harmless. In fact, he's such a wimp that he gets eaten by the female after mating. The female, on the other hand, is considered the most poisonous spider in the United States. If you are bitten, you will probably feel pain in the soles of your feet and your stomach, get very sweaty and develop swollen eyelids. The poison is 15 times more powerful than that of the prairie rattlesnake. Fortunately, black widows don't inject much of their poison so their bites are rarely fatal.

≪ 12 ≫
CROCODILE

Crocs and alligators may only have brains the size of cigars but they are the largest and most intelligent of all the reptiles. They can learn by watching you. For example, a croc will recognize a pattern in your behaviour if you come down to the water at the same time each day to swim or do your washing. However, crocs don't have very big appetites. Because they are cold-blooded and slow-moving, they can live on the same amount of food as a small bird! But if they *are* hungry they will attack just about anything that dares to approach the water!

« 11 »
BROWN RECLUSE SPIDER

As its name suggests, this spider is brown and doesn't much like company, preferring to hide out in the usual places you find spiders — bathrooms, bedrooms, wardrobes and basements. Brown recluse spiders are usually found in the southern and midwestern United States and most folks get stung by spiders hiding in clothes or towels that haven't been used for a while.

The brown recluse has three pairs of eyes arranged in a semicircle at the front of its head and a dark violin-shaped patch behind its eyes. It is highly poisonous and some people can have very severe reactions to its bite. First, a small white blister forms where you've been bitten, surrounded by a larger, swollen area. Within 36 hours you might develop a fever, feel sick and have aching joints. The spider's venom eats away flesh and you could end up with an open wound the size of your hand. Some people have taken months to recover from a bite and have even needed plastic surgery.

≪ 10 ≫
POLAR BEAR

They look big, fluffy and chilled out, but these giants of the Arctic have no natural predators. In other words, they are the hardest animals in their neighbourhood.

Adult males weigh about four times more than an adult male lion — that's about 635kg (100st), and they can smell dinner from 32km (20m) away. They can also run up to 40km/h (25mph) over short distances. Their favourite food is

seals, and they usually polish off one seal a week.

Humans rarely get attacked by adult males because the males are experienced hunters. It's the inexperienced younger polar bears and mothers with cubs that you need to watch out for. Despite its size, a polar bear can creep up on you from behind and you wouldn't even know it was there until it attacked.

« 9 »
CONE SHELL

"Cone shell" is a polite name for "Australian killer snail". Yes, killer snails really exist! All cone shells, of which there are about 500 different kinds worldwide, stab their prey with venom. Most of these snails hunt worms and other snails, but some of them are mad and bad enough to take on fish. The venom from some of these fish-killers is powerful enough to kill a human. These little gastropods literally harpoon their prey with hollow barbed tubes. Once they have struck their target, they pump venom into the victim, which dies almost immediately.

Cone shells are often very colourful and pretty but should never be picked up. There are reported cases of people who, after being stung, described a tingling feeling in their lips — just before they lapsed into a coma and died . . .

‹‹ 8 ››
BLACK MAMBA

The black mamba is the most feared snake in Africa and one of the most deadly snakes in the world. Just two drops of its venom can kill a human in a matter of minutes.

Most mambas are bright green, but the black mamba is olive to black. An adult can grow 1.5–3m (5–9ft) long and travel quite fast – at around 16km/h (10mph). It slithers along the ground with its head held high. Before it strikes, it lifts its head even higher, flattens its neck and flicks out its tongue. Once it has killed its prey, it can dislocate its bottom jaw to allow it to swallow whole animals up to four times the size of its own head.

≪ 7 ≫
KING COBRA

This is the biggest of all venomous snakes, growing up to 5m (16ft) long. It lives in India and Southeast Asia and is very dangerous. Just under 60ml (2fl oz) of its venom is enough to kill an elephant or 20 people within minutes. Its scientific name *Ophiophagus hannah* means "snake-eater", so even if you're another snake you still aren't safe from the king. It famously rears up and puffs out its neck before it strikes, and in this position can stand nearly 2m (6ft) tall!

« 6 »
SEA WASP

The sea wasp isn't an insect but a jellyfish. Its other name is the box jelly and it is extremely poisonous. A brush from one of its tentacles is enough to cause agonizing pain, vomiting and breathing problems.

The sea wasp's bell can grow as large as a basketball but the harmful parts are the tentacles, which can trail up to 5m (16ft) in the water. The tentacles are practically invisible because they are so thin and delicate, so although you might spot the bell of the jellyfish several metres (feet) away, you may be swimming right into its tentacles without even knowing it.

The whole length of each tentacle is armed with poison darts, which are chemically triggered to fire when they touch fish scales or skin. However, defending yourself from attack is possible using a simple trick — wearing women's tights. Australian lifeguards sometimes wear tights over their arms and legs because the nylon stops the poison darts being triggered.

≪ 5 ≫
BLUE-RINGED OCTOPUS

If you ever see the blue rings of this cute little yellow-brown octopus while you are swimming, you will probably be dead within five minutes. This is because the blue rings only appear just before it strikes!

The blue-ringed octopus is the world's most poisonous octopus and it is no bigger than a golf ball. It has poisonous spit, which is kept in two glands the same size as its brain. One of the glands contains poison, which it uses to kill its prey (such as crabs), and is harmless to humans. The second gland, however, contains a deadly nerve toxin, which it uses for defence. There is no known antidote. If you are bitten, you will be

blind and paralysed within seconds and dead within minutes. The only possibility of survival is hours of heart massage and artificial respiration while the poison works its way out of your system.

《《 4 》》
POISON DART FROG

Have you heard the phrase "you are what you eat"? Well, this little South American frog is no exception. It can produce some of the most toxic poison in the animal world, which it collects through eating certain bugs.

Poison dart frogs are usually bright red, orange or yellow and are only 2–5cm ($\frac{3}{4}$–2in) long. A single drop of their nerve poison is enough to kill a human. For centuries, many South American Indian communities have harvested the poison to tip the end of their arrows and blowpipe darts. Scientists estimate that the poison contains more than 300 powerful alkaloids (similar to cocaine and morphine), which may be useful in medical research.

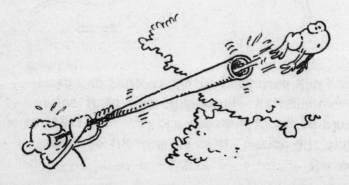

«« 3 »»
STONEFISH

The most poisonous fish in the world is one that sits on the seabed, minding its own business and looking like anything but a fish! In fact, distinguishing the stonefish from an encrusted rock is almost impossible. The stonefish doesn't go hunting for human flesh but it has 13 highly poisonous spines on its back that severely injure anyone who treads on them.

The Australian Aborigines act out an ancient ritual dance warning of the danger of stepping on a stonefish. In it, a man wades into the water looking for fish and steps on something that makes him scream in pain until his death at the end of the dance. The moral of this is "never take a stone at face value" — it could be a killer.

≪ 2 ≫
TYRANT LIZARD KING

This enormous animal can grow up to 12m (39ft) long and 6m (20ft) tall and weigh anything up to 6 tonnes (tons). It has 60 razor-sharp teeth, which are each 23cm (9in) long. It is very smart, can run up to 48km/h (30mph), and could rip an elephant apart in seconds. What a good job it has been dead for more than 145 million years!

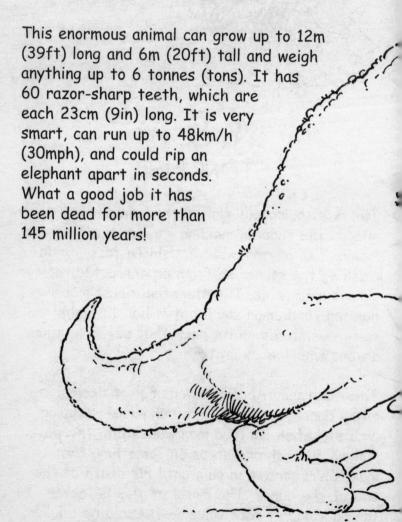

Yes, we're talking about Tyrannosaurus rex. (Who said that the **DUNG Top 20** animal killers have to be alive!)

《 1 》
MICROBES

Microbes lead a double life. Some of them are our number one friends — no life on Earth could exist without them — but some are our biggest enemies. Microbes are the smallest and oldest form of life on Earth and have existed for billions of years. When they do us harm, we call them GERMS.

The smallest and simplest microbes are viruses, which are just balls of genes wrapped in a shell, a millionth of a centimetre (inch) across.

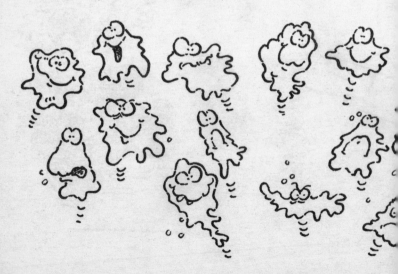

They reproduce by injecting themselves into other cells to produce thousands of new viruses. Viruses are very hard to fight because they constantly mutate into different strains. Bacteria are also microbes, but they are much larger than viruses. It's funny that we humans think these small things are all the same, but there's a whole world we can't see without a microscope. If a virus were the size of a human, a bacterium would be the size of the Statue of Liberty!

Then there are other microbes called protozoa. These are a 1,000 times larger than bacteria and the most recent. (They've only been on Earth for about 1.8 billion years!)

Finally, did you know that fungi — mushrooms, toadstools, mould and mildew — are microbes, too? In fact, microbes are EVERYWHERE. Here are a few of the good ones:

Lactobacillus acidophilus (lack-toe-bah-sill-us acid-off-ill-us) — turns milk into yoghurt.

Saccharomyces cerevisiae (sack-arrow-my-seas sair-uh-vis-ee-ay) — a yeast that makes bread rise.

Pseudomonas putida (sue-doe-moan-us poo-tea-dah) — eats sewage and helps to turn it into drinking water.

Escherichia coli (Esh-er-ish-e-ah coal-eye) — lives in your gut (with many other kinds of microbe) and helps you digest food.

Bad microbes, on the other hand, have been responsible for spreading all the world's infection and disease since the beginning of time.

Want to read more weird and wonderful stuff? Turn over to find out what kind of gross tricks many animals can play with their bodies.

CHAPTER THREE
WEIRD BODY STUFF

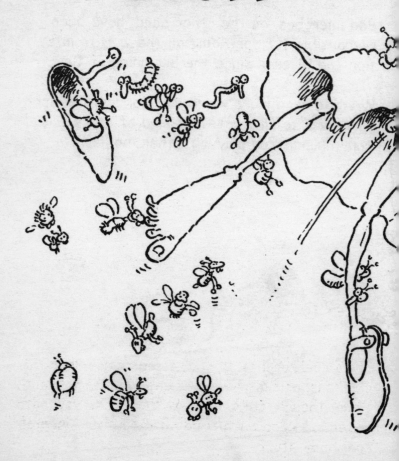

From cockroaches to chameleons and camels to chickens, animals have amazing bodies. Some of them, though, can do things that make your skin crawl . . . Read on to find out about all kinds of cool body stuff.

DON'T LOSE YOUR HEAD!

Snakes and reptiles are always game for a few gross body tricks. For example, if you cut off the head of an attacking rattlesnake it will carry on attacking you with its headless stump. Even if you move, the stump, which acts like it can "see", will still follow you around.

A salamander, which is a type of lizard, can even grow new body parts. If it loses its tail, a limb, or even an eye, it simply grows a new one.

Another lizard, called the stump-tailed chameleon, confuses its enemies because its tail looks like its head. When a predator attacks its tail, thinking it's going for the vulnerable head, the chameleon escapes by simply breaking it off. Then it runs away and grows another one.

BLOW-UP

There's another type of lizard, called the chuckwalla, which escapes danger by crawling into a crack in a rock. It wedges itself in place by inflating its body with air and cannot be pulled out.

THE WRIGGLER

The freakiest reptile performance has to be that of Pallas's glass snake, which is a legless lizard about 1.5m (5ft) long. When attacked, its body breaks into little pieces, which start wriggling in all directions. This allows the piece with the head to make its getaway while the confused attacker chases after all the other bits (or perhaps just bends over and barfs in disgust).

WHAT A BLAST!

The basilisk lizard has a really cool way of escaping predators and having a blast at the same time. It lives in trees, near water, and its webbed toes and sprinting talent allow it to walk (or rather, run) on water, at speeds up to 12km/h (7mph). It can cross lakes 400m wide (1,310ft) in this way. Talk about the power of positive thinking!

OK, if you think a lizard walking on water is amazing, how about a fish that can walk without water, or one that can fly like a bird?
Read on . . .

LANDED FISH

The clarius, or "walking catfish", lives in the
Florida Everglades. When its pond dries up, it
simply shrugs its fishy shoulders and sets off in
search of another pond, using its powerful tail
to push itself along the ground. It breathes on
land using special air-filled sacs leading from its
gills which act as primitive lungs.

FLYING FISH

A hatchetfish, which lives in South American rivers, can really fly. It has a huge chest, making it the only fish capable of flapping flight. It hurls itself out of the water and uses its tail and large pectoral fins to fly for several metres (feet) before splash-landing again.

MAD MYTH

Q: Which animal gets a date by doing press-ups?

A: Iguanas attract a mate by doing lots of macho press-ups and making all sorts of body postures. They have a wide range of fixed signals that they combine to convey a variety of messages, such as "Look at my pecs" and "I don't think much of yours". Stuck for birthday present ideas for your pet iguana? How about a tiny pair of leopard-print posing briefs and a mirror?

ANIMAL CONTORTIONISTS

You may have heard said that it's difficult for a camel to squeeze through the eye of a needle. You probably also know that cats use their whiskers to judge whether they can fit through a gap or not. But did you know that a giant Pacific octopus can fit its entire body through a hole the size of its beak!

More worryingly, rats can get through holes no bigger than a penny. That's especially worrying for city-dwellers because it's said that in cities, there's always a rat within 5m (16ft) of you!

DUNG'S TOP 10 MOST COLOURFUL BUMS

1 Mandrill (the monkey with the blue-and-red bum)
2 Peacock (multicoloured)
3 Baboon (red)
4 Waterbuck (has a white ring around it)
5 Imperial shrimp (bright red)
6 Chameleon (sometimes)
7 Flamingo (pink from a carotene-rich diet)
8 . . . er I can't think of any more. Does an elephant with piles count?

Q: Which animal has a grandfather but no father?

A: This is a tough one. The answer is a drone, which is a male bee.

Drones hatch from unfertilized bee eggs. Fertilized eggs turn into either workers (infertile females) or queens (fertile females).

Imagine a drone called Henry who gets together with a queen bee called Queeny. If one of the eggs that Henry fertilizes turns into another queen (Queeny Junior) and Queeny Junior gets together with another drone called Nigel, then any of Queeny Junior's eggs that Nigel doesn't fertilize will become drones – which are Henry's grandchildren, but not Nigel's children. In other words, these drones have a grandfather called Henry but no father.

Ah, you say, but what about those eggs that Henry didn't fertilize? Well, they turn into drones. So, you say, Henry must be their father. But Henry isn't their father, that's the point, because those are the eggs that Henry didn't fertilize. Confusing, eh?

HALL OF FAME

Miracle Mike

Chickens are known for running around for up to an hour after their heads have been chopped off. It's very strange to watch, but it doesn't mean that the chicken is "alive" in the sense of thinking and feeling — it's a muscle response thing.

A chicken called Mike became a celebrity around the west coast of the United States after refusing to call it a day. On 10 September 1945, the chicken's owner, Lloyd Owen, chopped off its head with the intention of cooking it for dinner that very evening. The chicken, however, had other ideas. Although his head was completely severed from his body, he continued to strut around as if nothing had happened. He balanced on his perch, he crowed (by making a strange gurgling sound in his throat), and he even tried to preen himself with his nonexistent head.

After a few days, the chicken was clearly not going to take his decapitation lying down and soon his fame spread. "Miracle Mike", as he became known, started touring the west coast, with people paying just 25 cents a time to see him. Soon, other local chicken owners started chopping the heads off some of *their* chickens, hoping to cash in on Mike's amazing success. One copycat chicken called Lucky managed to survive for 11 days without his head before bashing into a stovepipe and dying. Several other headless chickens lived for a few days.

So what was Mike's secret? Well, scientists who examined him confirmed that he was indeed minus one head. They also discovered that part of his brain (called the brain stem) was still intact, enabling him to continue to function on a very basic level. A blood clot prevented him from bleeding to death and his caring owner (!)

used an eyedropper to feed him a mixture of milk and water daily through his open throat.

Miracle Mike was eventually done in by his favourite food — he choked on a kernel of corn, an incredible four years later!

Every year his home town, Fruita, honours his memory with a special holiday. On 17 May 1999, they held the first "Mike the Headless Chicken Day" in tribute to one of its most celebrated citizens! Events included the "Run like a Headless Chicken Race", "Pin the Head on the Chicken", and a "Strut Your Stuff Chicken Dance"!

INCREDIBLE IMPRESSIONS

Some animals get their kicks out of doing weird impressions. These either allow them to sneak up on their lunch, or help them to avoid being on another animal's lunch menu.

Copycat king

For example, the king snake is harmless but nobody messes with it because its red, yellow and black stripes make it look just like a coral snake, which is poisonous and mean! In the same way, the gopher snake can hiss like a rattlesnake and even rattle its tail against dry leaves to freak out its attacker.

Sneaky sphinx

When the caterpillar of the sphinx moth sees danger, the front part of its body and its head swell up and its eyes bulge. This, together with its peculiar markings, makes it look just like a dangerous snake.

Star turn

The eastern hognose snake is not only a top impressionist but also deserves an animal Oscar for acting. Its first line of defence is to puff up its head to make it look like a king cobra. If this doesn't work, it writhes around on the ground with its tongue lolling out of the corner of its mouth to fake its own gruesome death. It even makes itself smell like a dead snake, too. In fact, it would probably even stick its legs up in the air, too, if it had any!

Talented twigs

The tawny frogmouth bird from Australia looks like a boring old twig, and the African tree-hopper (an insect) looks like a thorn. If a bunch of tree-hoppers hang out on a twig they look like a prickly branch.

Katydids, which are related to grasshoppers and crickets, live in the Venezuelan part of the Amazon rainforest. They escape danger by looking like leaves in various stages of decay, complete with veins and spots.

Frog poo

Best of all, though, is the Ecuador tree frog. This delightful creature pulls off a truly gross impersonation of a pile of bird poo, causing casual observers and predators alike to exclaim, "Ugh! Look at that bird poo!" and give it a wide berth.

DRESSED CRAB

There's a type of crab that doesn't do impressions, but does like dressing up and has earned itself the name of decorator crab. That doesn't mean that you'll find it laying carpet or putting up wallpaper. It gets its name from its habit of adorning itself with seaweed, sponges and bits of coral. This helps it blend into the scenery, making it harder for its predators to spot it — and harder for them to eat it if they do.

DON'T MESS WITH ME!

Some animals are just too mean to waste time on impressions. When attacked, they get straight down to business. The horned lizard from North America freaks out anything that tries to mess with it. If it is being eaten, it squirts blood out of its eyes. The blood tastes so horrible that the attacker drops the lizard out of its mouth in disgust.

Soldier nasute termites have nozzle-shaped heads that allow them to shoot globs of itchy glue at their attackers. The glue is a bit like tree sap and very unpleasant for the unfortunate creature that gets in the firing line.

The bombardier beetle covers its attackers with a burning hot acid. It carries explosive chemicals around in its abdomen which only mix when the beetle is provoked, otherwise the beetle would blow itself to bits. When a predator gets too close, the chemicals heat up to 100°C (221°F) and shoot out with a loud bang and even smoke.

TELL ME WHY

Q: Can sheep shear themselves?

A: Yes! Australian sheep farmers are experimenting with a process called biological wool harvesting. They inject the sheep with a special protein that stops the wool under their skin growing for just 24 hours. This creates a break in each strand of wool. After about a month, the break reaches the surface of the skin, allowing the fleece to peel off in one perfect piece. This makes the fleece more valuable and saves time and money!

TELL ME WHY

Q: Which animal shoots poison darts out of its bum?

A: The sea cucumber, which looks like a pickle with spikes, is found in all the world's oceans. When a crab or a crayfish attacks it, it shoots poisonous tubes out of its bum. Some really gross sea cucumbers shoot their entire digestive systems out of their behinds before they scurry away.

JOKE CORNER

What is red and green and runny?
A frog in a blender.

Why do giraffes have such big nostrils?
Have you seen the size of their fingers?

What do you get if you cross an elephant with a ton of prunes?
Out of the way.

TOOTHY TALES

Some animals can do great stunts with their teeth — especially predators, such as sharks and crocodiles.

New gnashers
Sharks and crocs are always losing teeth when they attack other animals. A shark can grow a new set of teeth in a week and a croc can grow up to 50 new sets of teeth in a lifetime (which may explain why it doesn't bother to floss regularly).

Tooth travel
Dolphins use their teeth to help find their way around. Most people know that they use sound ("echolocation") to navigate. However, scientists also believe that the dolphin's teeth are an important part of this system and fine-tune its ability to pick up and interpret sounds.

A powerful bite
Rodents' teeth never stop growing but they are always being worn down by all that gnashing and gnawing! In fact, a rat's teeth are so strong it can bite through aluminium, lead and other metals.

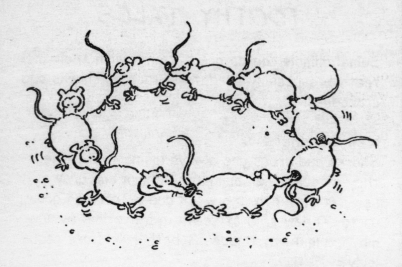

Bum biters

Some animals have teeth where you wouldn't
expect to find them. For example, baby shrews
sometimes have teeth in their bums. How? Well,
when the mother shrew takes her newborn
babies out of the burrow, instead of holding
hands, they bite down on the backside of the
shrew walking in front. That way, they all stay
together and none get lost. An Austrian shrew
biologist once removed the mother from the
front of a line of these bum-munchers to see
what would happen next. The shrew at the front
of the line bit on the backside of the last in
the line and they just walked around in a big
circle!

Toothy tools

Animal teeth have always been popular among humans. Over the years, we have used them for all sorts of things, such as currency and weapons. The teeth of the red-bellied piranha are so sharp that some South American Indians use them to make razors and scissors.

TOP TONGUE FACTS

- The chameleon's tongue is as long as its tail and body put together!

- Crocodiles can't stick out their tongues!

- At 90cm (35in) long, the giraffe has one of the longest tongues in the animal world.

- A blue whale's tongue is the same size and weight as a full-grown African elephant.

- A giraffe's tongue is blue.

- A gorilla sticks out its tongue to express anger.

- The South American anteater's long, sticky tongue grows up to 60cm (24in) in length. It uses it to catch ants and can eat more than 30,000 a day.

- The emperor moth begins life with a nice juicy tongue but by the time it has grown into an adult its tongue has shrunk away to nothing. Eventually, the moth is unable to feed and dies of starvation.

Q: Where does the blood for animal blood transfusions come from?

A: From other animals. Yes, animals, like humans, often require blood transfusions during operations and they receive blood from other donor animals. Many countries have blood banks for animals as well as for humans, and you can nominate your own pet as a blood donor.

Dogs have about 12 different blood types and horses have more than 15 different blood types, so

it's not always as easy to come up with a match
as it is for humans. If vets can't find a match
they can use artificial blood products instead. For
example, "oxyglobin" is an artificial blood product
derived from cattle blood.

If this all sounds a bit weird, then did you know
that the closest thing in chemical composition to
your own blood is seawater? In fact, many tropical
marine fish could survive in a tank filled with
human blood!

TELL ME WHY

GIVE BLOOD TODAY

SKINLESS WONDERS

When animals aren't growing new bits and losing old ones, many just can't resist shedding their skins. If you think the bath looks scaly after your dad has been in it, then just think about newts! In fact, a newt has smooth, shiny skin but this is only because it sheds its old, wrinkly skin. When the old layer of skin starts to split around the newt's mouth, it uses its fingers to peel the skin off in one piece, like a mask.

Imagine if you were watching television with your granny and she suddenly did that. It would freak you out, wouldn't it? Perhaps it's quite addictive, though, like peeling flaky skin if you've got sunburnt on holiday.

By the way, we're not the only animals that can stay out in the sun too long. A dog's nose, pigs and beluga whales can easily get burnt in the sun, too. Hippos manage to avoid getting burnt by producing their own sun cream. They secrete a pink fluid which dries to form a protective coating over their thin, delicate skin.

MAD MYTH

Spotted horses are magical.

ALL ABOUT COCKROACHES

There's a lot to say about cockroaches because they're gross AND amazing. They should be — they've been practising their gross behaviour for more than 400 million years, which means they've been around more than a hundred times longer than we humans.

There are about 3,500 known species of cockroach in the world today and they come in all sizes and colours. The largest roach lives in South America and is 15cm (6in) long with a 30-cm (12-in) wingspan. Imagine finding one of those hiding in your shoe!

Cockroaches are fast, too. They can fly up to 50 body lengths per second. This means that if a 1.8m (6ft) roach entered the Olympic Games, it would break the world record in the 100m final in eight seconds and be collecting its gold medal before the other runners were out of the starting blocks.

And what's more, you could chop off its head and it would still win! Yes, a cockroach can survive for a whole week without its head and

then it would only die because it couldn't drink any water. A cockroach's brain isn't just in its head, it's spread throughout its whole body.

Surely that's enough amazing skill for any one type of insect but there's more. Have you ever crunched a cockroach? The white stuff that oozes out of its body is fat — the roach's energy store. This fat helps the roach treat or dispose of any insecticides it may encounter. That's why cockroaches are so difficult to kill.

TOP COCKROACH FACTS

- They have 18 knees (3 on each leg) so they'd easily win a knobbly knee competition.

- They can hold their breath for 40 minutes and they can swim. (So if a giant roach jumps into your bath, don't try to swim away!)

- They bleed white blood.

- Their skeletons grow outside their bodies and are shed several times a year. You can tell when a roach has just shed its skin because it will have white skin and black eyes for the first eight hours before it regains its original colouring.

- Some female cockroaches mate just once then are pregnant for the rest of their lives.

- Their hearts can pump their blood forwards AND backwards around their bodies.

- They have a set of salivary glands and are pretty good at spitting.

- They are incredibly tough yet spend most of their lives resting, just hanging out under your fridge or in your bath. (Though only about 1 per cent of roaches lives indoors.)

Have you ever wondered what a day in the life of a roach might be like? Turn over to read an extract from the diary of Roger Roach.

In my own words by Roger Roach

4:30 a.m. Had a blast during the night. Did a 100 laps around the fridge just for a laugh — didn't even get out of breath. The sun's coming up. Time to chill out in my favourite spot — under the toaster. My exoskeleton feels a bit tight today. Have been meaning to shed it for ages. I suppose it can't wait any longer. What a hassle! I just feel like hanging out today. Still, dem bones have got to go . . .

7:15 a.m. Woke up to the smell of burning toast. Someone must be cooking breakfast. Sprinted away from the heat and smell and fell off the side of the table. No sweat. Then someone stamped on me. Again, no sweat. Scuttled under the refrigerator. Think I'll go back to sleep.

12:00 a.m. Woke up. Dreamt I was running in the Olympic Games, leaving the others standing. Got gold but then was disqualified for having too many knees. Bummer.

12:15 a.m. A small dust grolley has just blown under the fridge. Gave it a nudge with one of my antenna. No big deal.

3:00 p.m. HAVE JUST BEEN WOKEN UP AGAIN! The kid got back from school, opened the fridge and spilt a

carton of orange juice all over the floor. I swam
to safety and headed for the kid's shoes that he'd
kicked off at the door. That'll teach him. It's nice and
dark in here. Think I'll shed my exoskeleton. Oh yeah.
Mmmmmm.

5:00 p.m. I'm hungry. I'll wait until it gets dark, though,
before I go looking for food. I'm bored. Think I'll hold
my breath.

5:42 p.m. Haaaaaaaaaaaa. Phew. Beat . . . my record
. . . by two minutes . . . Cool . . .

7:15 p.m. Must have dozed off again. I'm really hungry
now. It should be dark outside . . .
Neeeuuurrgh! The kid has just stuck his cheesy foot
back into his shoe. Time to leave . . . Yum . . . his
skin tastes quite good. Oh no, now he knows there's
something in his shoe . . . tipping up . . . falling. Have
just hit the carpet. What's all the fuss? Stop screaming.
Have you never seen a roach before? Honestly . . .
people!

Q: Why don't woodpeckers get concussion?

A: The shock waves created when a woodpecker bashes its beak into a tree are transferred less easily into its head because it has a narrow space between its skull and its brain. The brain is protected by dense and spongy bone which cushions the impact. Some of the bird's neck muscles also contract to absorb and distribute the shock. The woodpecker closes its eyes just before impact. Well, wouldn't you close your eyes if you were about to bash your head against a tree?

Woody woodpecker's most important secret is its ability to hit a tree trunk absolutely straight. First it taps the wood gently to line up its head, just as someone hammering in a nail might tap the nail gently a couple of times before a big strike. Then it starts pecking the wood like crazy but never allows its head to twist. (Woodpeckers also have small brains which probably helps. Maybe if their brains were bigger they wouldn't go around head-butting trees in the first place.)

MAD MYTH

When a cat licks its fur the wrong way, bad weather is on the way.

CAMEL CRAZY

You either love them or hate them. They have a reputation for being temperamental, and they're always making heaving sounds like they are about to cough up a good globule of spit. However, they also tend to be good-natured, patient and intelligent.

Spit it out

The bit about the spit is true: camels can spit up to 200g (6oz) of gross phlegm with great force and accuracy. So remember, if your camel is making weird noises and moving his mouth a lot, stand well clear! There's even a name for the hocking noise that a camel makes. It's called "nuzzing".

Taking the heat

Above all, though, it's a camel's ability to withstand high temperatures and harsh desert
conditions that have made it so invaluable to
humans. The Bedouin name for the dromedary
(the camel with one hump) is "Ata Allah" which
means "Gift from God".

Camels don't pant or even sweat very much. In
fact, they can tolerate a rise in body temperature of as much as 6°C (42.8°F) before
sweating. That doesn't sound like much but we
humans get very uncomfortable if our body
temperature rises by just 1°C (33.8°F) and we
would die if it went up by 6°C (42.8°F).

Got the hump

A camel can go up to a week with no food or
water but when it drinks it can really knock it
back — around 100l (22g) in just 10 minutes!

A camel doesn't store this water in its hump.
The hump is a mound of fatty tissue from which
it draws energy when food is scarce. When a
camel uses its hump fat for sustenance, the
mound becomes floppy and shrinks. If a camel
uses up too much fat, the hump may even flop
down the camel's back. However, the hump soon
returns to normal after the camel has taken in
food and water.

Q: Why do irritating gnats always hover in big groups and why, when you walk through them or swipe them with your hand, do they regroup in the same place?

A: Gnats, by the way, is a general name for lots of species of tiny flies, especially fruit flies. The males swarm together in large groups while they wait for lady gnats to appear. As they only live for a few weeks (poor souls), it's not surprising that they regroup themselves quickly after you barge through them. So, next time you see some hopeful gnats swarming in the evening, spare a thought for them, and be sure to walk around them!

Animals have certainly developed some incredible tricks. In the next chapter you'll discover that they also have sensational senses. Turn over to read about some incredible animal powers that make we humans look like a sad and sorry bunch . . .

CHAPTER FOUR

SENSATIONAL SENSES

Let's face it: we think we humans are pretty cool. We reckon we've developed excellent senses over the few million years that we've been on this planet, and that none of the other animals really match us.

Well, we might be intelligent but when it comes to extraordinary senses the rest of the animal kingdom leave us way behind. Also, many animals seem to have a sixth sense, not just five. That's why many of them seem to know when there's a storm brewing, or an earthquake is about to strike. Lots of animals can also sense magnetic fields and electrical signals, which helps them to navigate and hunt for food.

SMELLS GOOD

Have you ever wished you had really smelly feet, so that you could find your way home by your scent when you're lost? Well, that's how deer do it. They produce musk oil from between their toes that leaves a musky trail to tell them where they've been.

Ants do something similar, laying down a chemical trail, so that they can constantly exchange smell information.

Cats and dogs also beat us noses down when it comes to smelling. Some people think that a dog's sense of smell is more than a million times more powerful than that of a human.

Mind you, this doesn't mean that dogs can smell everything better than us. Dogs can detect fatty acids like those in sweat with no problem, but tests have shown that they are not as well adapted as humans are to detecting sweet smells, such as vanilla and caraway.

An emperor moth can detect the smell of another moth from up to 5km (3m) away. Even fish can smell well. Some sharks can smell one part of blood in 100 million parts of water. A migratory fish's smell helps it to find its way home to mate — sometimes thousands of kilometres (miles) away.

Q: Can animals really smell fear?

A: I'm sure you have heard that many people believe that animals can smell fear. This belief, however, is not literally true although animals ARE particularly good at picking up on a variety of sight, sound and smell cues from other animals.

For example, if you were really scared of a dog you would sweat more (humans do sweat more when they're frightened) and the dog would probably smell your sweat. However, it would also pick up other signs that you were nervous – you might be fidgeting, or talking to yourself, and so on. These things would be just as likely to tell the dog that something was up. The dog would therefore detect a new smell, be alerted to "danger" and see you as a threat because of the way you smell and how you are behaving, but not because it thinks "I smell fear".

STRESSED-OUT SMELLS

Some animals, such as rats, mice, ants and bees, release smells when they are stressed. However, these smells mainly act as a warning to others that there is danger and do not make an enemy aggressive. In fact, the smell released by skunks, weasels and wolverines is so vile that it actually repels any attack!

Bee-have
If a honeybee detects an intruder in or near its hive, it will release an alarm smell that attracts other bees to the spot. Therefore, if you are frightened of bees, they will not gather around and attack you because they smell your sweat. Instead, they will gather around you because the alarm smell has been set off and only attack you because of your subsquent behaviour – such as screaming and waving your arms around in a blind panic!

'EAR 'EAR

Do you want proof that some animals have much better hearing than us? Well, humans can hear sounds that range between 20 and 20,000 Hz — that's equivalent to the lowest and highest notes of a church organ — but look at these amazing hearing test results:

Human	20–20,000 Hz
Cat	100–60,000 Hz
Dog	up to 40,000 Hz
Elephant	1–20,000 Hz
Grasshopper	up to 50,000 Hz
Mice	1,000–100,000 Hz
Noctuid moth	1,000–240,000 Hz
Rat	1,000–90,000 Hz

Now who would have thought that rodents and insects have better hearing than us?

SHARP EARS

The animal with the best hearing is probably the owl, which can hear a mouse stepping on a twig up to 20m (65ft) away. However, the Californian leaf-nosed bat can actually hear the footsteps of insects, which is quite impressive, too.

BIG EARS

And take a look at what elephants can hear.
Their hearing is about the same as ours at the
top of the range but they can also hear way
down low (called "infra sound"), which is why
they can detect earthquakes and storms
brewing.

A pigeon can hear very low-pitched sounds, too.
It could be hundreds of kilometres (miles) away
from the sea and still detect the sound of
waves breaking on the shore. With hearing that
good, how do pigeons sleep at night?

MAD MYTH

MOVING EARS

Some animals have their hearing tackle in weird places. Cicadas have it on their stomach, while crickets sport a delightful pair of ears on their knees.

Of course, lots of animals can move their ears, too, while most of us can't even twitch ours. For example, dogs have 17 muscles in their ears so that they can turn them in any direction.

Q: Do fish grunt?

A: Well, it would be a boring world if there wasn't a grunting fish somewhere . . . and sure enough, the freshwater *Aplodinotus grunniens* ("grunter") is as good as its name. The male has a special set of muscles, which it vibrates to produce a grunting, drumming sound. Why? Well, as with lots of strange animal behaviour, it impresses the female of the same species who can't resist a hefty grunter – in fact, the gruntier the better. So if you're fishing and you catch a silvery fish that starts croaking like a bullfrog when you take it out of the water, you know you've caught a grunter.

BAT-TASTIC

All bats are incredible. Like dolphins, they use echolocation to find their way around, even in complete darkness. They emit a very high-pitched and loud pulse of ultrasound about $1/1000$th of a second long. The sound they make is so loud that if it wasn't above the range of our own hearing, we'd find it extremely uncomfortable. In fact, to prevent the bat from deafening itself its ear bones pull away from the eardrum at just the right moment!

Blind as a bat?

The bat picks up the echoes from the pulse of ultrasound and its brain turns the information into a "picture" of its surroundings. This picture is so detailed that a bat can distinguish distances and different surface textures to within a fraction of a millimetre (inch). This gives it a better understanding of its surroundings than we get of ours using our eyes, so the phrase "blind as a bat" is definitely a misconception. Bats can't "see" in the same way that we can, but their brains can make much better use of the echolocation information than our brains can from what our eyes "see".

Scientists are exploring echolocation as a way to help visually impaired people, but even using modern supercomputers they can't come close to reproducing the sophistication and sensitivity of the bat's super-senses.

MAD MYTH

If a bat lands on your head, it won't fly away until it hears thunder.

JOKE CORNER

What do you call a cow with no legs?
Ground beef.

What is black and white and red all over?
A Dalmatian with sunburn.

What's white and green and hops across the table?
A frog sandwich.

What's white and green and doesn't move?
Half a frog sandwich.

What's small and cuddly and blue?
A koala holding his breath.

How do you make a tortoise fast?
Don't feed it for two months.

SEEING IS BELIEVING

This is where we really come a cropper because animals can both see more clearly and more widely than us.

Get down on all fours now. Go on. Put the book down and pretend you've got four legs. Are you kneeling comfortably? OK, if you were a donkey, right now you'd be able to see all four feet at the same time — very important if you've got twice as many legs as we have to trip over.

Right. Now let's try another little experiment. Look to your right and focus on an object. Keeping your right eye fixed on that spot, move your left eye to look at something else, something over there on your left. Don't move your right eye, just your left!

Impossible, you cry! Well, chameleons and seahorses can do it. Their eyes can move independently so they can see in two different directions at the same time! (This is particularly useful if you want to avoid being eaten.)

FOUR EYES

Did you know that there's a fish called the "four-eyed fish" that can see in air and water simultaneously. Flaps divide each of its eyes, one flap opening in the air and the other in the water. This means the fish can float at the water's surface and look up and down at the same time.

Scallops can see all around, too. They have about 100 eyes positioned around the edge of their shells, so they can spot a predator coming from any direction.

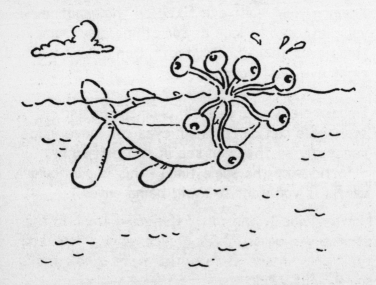

MAD MYTH

No one ever sees a dead donkey. If you do see a dead donkey, leaping over its carcass three times will bring you good luck.

BIRD'S EYE VIEW

It's the birds of prey that have the best eyesight, though. They can spot a small rodent on the ground when they are flying more than 4,570m (15,000ft) in the air! Next time you're in an aeroplane and the pilot announces that you're cruising at 4,570m (15,000ft), look out of the window and try to spot a car on the ground, never mind a rodent. You'll soon realize what incredible birds they are.

Now imagine trying to do the same thing in the dark. Some birds of prey, such as owls, can see their prey in almost total darkness — now that's some night vision!

Big eye

Have you heard the saying that the eyes are the gateway to the soul? Well, for the giant squid they're more like manhole covers. Each of its huge eyes measures a staggering 25cm (10in) in diameter!

Q: Is it true that swans can allow one half of their brain to sleep while the other half is awake?

A: A lot of birds have this ability. Scientists call it "unihemisphere slow-line sleep" – I call it kipping with one eye open. What happens is that the part of the brain linked to the open eye keeps awake (although very relaxed) while the other half of the brain sleeps. That way, birds can keep a lookout for predators while they sleep. Aquatic mammals, such as dolphins, can also do this. In fact, dolphins would drown if they didn't because if both sides of their brains slept at the same time, they wouldn't keep returning to the surface to breathe.

A QUESTION OF TASTE

There are plenty of animals that have unquestionably better taste than us, too. A catfish, for instance, has more than 100,000 taste buds. Pigs have around 15,000 and rabbits around 17,000. We humans have a measly 8,000.

Good taste

Some animals sense taste in weird places, too. A butterfly tastes with its feet, and so does a blowfly, which has around 3,000 sensitive hairs on its feet. So remember, if you want good taste, why not grow some hair on your toes!

Very Touchy

Many animals have a highly developed sense of touch and a cat is an amazing example of this. It's not just a cat's whiskers that are super sensitive. Scattered within its fur are single hairs called tylotrichs that are just as sophisticated. Its skin contains millions of touch receptors that can detect the tiniest changes in pressure, air currents and temperature. Its paws are packed with receptors which help it to judge the texture and density of its prey. So if you think cats can be very touchy, you'd be right!

Sixth Sense

Animals have been known to behave strangely before earthquakes and other natural disasters, possibly because their heightened senses allow them to pick up clues that we can't. An elephant might sense an earthquake because it can hear very low sounds, whereas a cat would be able to pick up minute vibrations through its feet. So pay attention to your pets — they may know something you don't!

Yes, I think you'll agree that animals win hands down when it comes to the senses. Don't be disappointed, though. In fact, you may actually be pleased that they come out top when it comes to poop. Turn to the next chapter to find out more . . .

CHAPTER FIVE
POOP!

No book about animal grossology would be complete without an in-depth analysis of . . . well, let's just say that we've all heard of the saying "What goes in must come out"!

In this chapter you'll discover that animals are expert at producing, reusing or simply rolling around in the stuff. Yes, you've guessed it — poop!

TOP TRUMPS

Bet you didn't know that dairy cows can produce up to 450l (99g) of farts and burps a day. That's 50 million tonnes (tons) a year. With an estimated 1.2 billion cattle in the whole world, that's an awful lot of methane.

So what's their secret? Well, the fact that they only eat grass is the key to their mega-flatulence. That and being much bigger than people, of course. All the same, it's a quite impressive bottom-burping record.

MAD MYTH

Methane is the second most important greenhouse gas after carbon dioxide and is thought to be responsible for about 20 per cent of the greenhouse effect.

The only human being who has ever come close to a cow's impressive bottom control was a Frenchman called Joseph Pagnol. (Skip to Chapter eight for full details of this amazing fartiste.)

The whiff of a whale's spout, or blow, causes brain disorders. (Sailors used to believe this because it has such a strong and foul smell.)

PUMPING POWER

To be serious for a moment, there's enormous untapped potential in the power of cow farts. Researchers at the Department of Highways in Forth Worth, Texas, United States, have worked out that the cow population exudes more than 50 million tonnes (tons) of gas into the atmosphere just from burping.

If we could find a way of capturing this valuable natural resource, then as few as 10 cows could heat and light a small house per year! That's no joke.

Chicken dung is used in southeast England as a source of energy. More than 200,000 tonnes (tons) of chicken poop is collected every year from around 70 million chickens and is burnt to create enough electricity for 12,000 homes. Now that's poop power!

PRICELESS POOP

Animal poop can actually be very valuable stuff. Fossilized bird droppings are one of the main exports of Nauru, an island in the Western Pacific. The poo is rich in phosphates and is used in fertilizer.

WHAT A GAS!

Which animals do you think produce the most gas? Have a guess — killer whales, elephants, hippos? Wrong! The answer is termites. Together, termites are responsible for creating the largest amount of methane out of all the world's animals. OK, so each little termite doesn't produce much gas on its own. However, if you were to put all the world's animals into one big pile, around 20 per cent of the heap would consist of termites.

Mind you, that's not to say that elephants don't produce a lot of poop. They do. Just one elephant poops more than 20kg (44lb) a day!

And whales? Well, if a whale weighs about the same as 30 elephants . . . *you* do the sums! And to think that all whales eat are microscopic plants and animals.

A CASE OF THE RUNS

Some animals have no control over their bodily functions at all. Take koala bears, for instance. They look so cute and cuddly yet they are totally incontinent. The same is true of mice, and you don't want to know what flamingos do . . . Well, all right. Just like the turkey vulture, flamingos pee down their very long legs. The urine then evaporates and helps to cool them down.

MAD MYTH

It is good luck if a bird poops on your car.

Q: Why do dogs drag their butts along the floor?

A: If your dog does this, then it is suffering from "flop bot" and you should get it to the vet. It happens when the special doggy scent glands in the dog's bum (which it uses for marking out its territory) have become blocked and swollen with vile-smelling fluid. The infection makes the dog's backside unbearably itchy, which is why it slaps its bum on the ground, sticks its legs around its ears and heaves itself along the ground to have a good scratch.

TELL ME WHY

HALL OF FAME
The Thisbe Irenea caterpillar

When a Thisbe Irenea caterpillar is attacked by an Ichneumen wasp in the jungles of Costa Rica, it drums for help and an army of friendly ants springs to its rescue. The ants then fight off the wasp by squirting acid at it and they save the caterpillar's life. Why do the ants help in this way?

The gruesome truth is that the ants just love to eat the caterpillar's faeces because it contains vital minerals and forms an essential part of their diet. They are therefore happy to be the caterpillar's bodyguards to safeguard supplies of the precious poop.

Q: Do fish fart?

A: Many fish have something called a swim bladder which they inflate with air and then deflate to control their buoyancy. Usually, they burp out excess gas from the swim bladder. The sand tiger shark, however, gulps air into its stomach at the water's surface then farts out the excess to sink. Since farting comes from the digestive system, this behaviour does probably qualify as farting. However, some experts believe that any gases produced as by-products of digestion get absorbed and compressed into poop so, technically, fish don't fart or produce an air biscuit (or should I say water biscuit) at all. With all that compressed gas in their poop, I wonder if fish poo would taste fizzy . . . Hmmmmm, I bet there's a scientist somewhere who knows the answer!

If you want to get even more techy, one theory says that coral-eating fish ought to do killer farts. To explain this, we need the help of a little chemistry. Coral is made up of calcium carbonate. Stomachs are usually filled with acid. Mix the two together and you should get lots and lots of fizzy stuff, or carbon dioxide. So next time you see all those beautiful brightly coloured fish on a nature documentary, you'll know they hide a guilty secret!

Finally, at the very least, herring should hold up their fins and say "guilty as charged" when it comes to dropping a chalupa. To escape predators, a whole shoal of herring do something called "sounding" which means that they all swim downwards very quickly to escape predators and fishing nets. But what they do next has to win them the award for fishy flatulence. They all let rip simultaneously to create an enormous rising bubble of guff that rushes to the surface to confuse their predators. Presumably it also helps them to sink faster as well.

So there you have it. The jury is still out on some species of fish but let's hear it for farting sharks and butt-burping herring!

POOP WARS

Lots of animals have discovered that covering themselves in their own poo can deter would-be predators. Others just throw the stuff at their attackers — not very subtle, but it often works.

Revolting rear

Female tortoise beetles resort to a truly gross secret weapon. They have a prickly structure on their backsides that gets clogged with dead skin and faeces. Any predator that attacks them is in for a nasty shock because the beetle rubs its revolting rear in the predator's face. The beetle then makes its escape while the predator is wiping away this smelly lump of vile goo.

Poison poop

Some beetles that use their poop as a defence also have poisonous poop.

Deadly dung

The larvae of the three-lined potato beetle push their excrement (called frass) on to their backs. This puts off would-be attackers because the larvae's diet includes a plant called night-shade, which is poisonous to predators.

In the name of science

There is a scientist in the United States who studies the chemicals in this beetle poop. First, though, he has to collect it by scraping it off their backs. He must be the only person in the world who earns a living by scraping poop from the backs of beetle larvae. His job even has a name — he's a fecologist.

DINO DUNG

Other scientists spend their whole careers looking for and examining very old poop — so old, in fact, that it has become fossilized. A coprolite is the name for fossilized dinosaur droppings and they are quite common. Imagine how much poo a Tyrannosaurus or Diplodocus must have produced — probably enough to bury a person. You wouldn't want to be standing under one of those babies when they were doing their business.

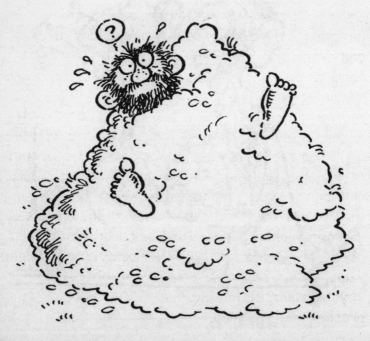

A precious pile

Scientists can learn lots from looking at
dinosaur droppings, such as what dinosaurs ate
and drank and how they digested their food. A
team of palaeontologists have just found a prime
specimen in Saskatchewan, Canada. It is a
whitish-green rock 44cm (17in) long, 15cm (6in)
high and 13cm (5in) wide, and the palaeontologists are really excited because it is the largest
coprolite ever found from a meat-eater and the
only one from a Tyrannosaurus. They have even
worked out that the coprolite contains chunks
of bone from a plant-eating dinosaur which must
have been eaten by the Tyrannosaurus 65 million
years ago! A replica is now an exhibit at the
Royal Saskatchewan Museum. That is one
precious pile of poop.

JOKE CORNER

What do you call a fly with no wings?
A walk.

A hare-raising tale . . .
A man was driving along a road when a rabbit jumped out in front of his car. The man slammed on his brakes and swerved, but still he hit the rabbit. He jumped out of his car and to his horror found that the little animal was dead. He was so upset that he began to cry. Soon, a woman stopped her car and asked him what had happened. He explained that he had been unable to stop in time and had just run over and killed a rabbit.

"Don't worry," said the woman, "I have something in my car which will sort him out." She went back to her car and returned with a spray can. She sprayed the dead rabbit all over until suddenly it leaped up and hopped away. Then it stopped and waved, then hopped off again. Finally it waved its paw at them one more time then disappeared into some bushes. "That's incredible," said the man. "What's in that can?" The woman turned the can around so that he could read the label. It said: "HARE SPRAY: RESTORES LIFE TO DEAD HARE. ADDS PERMANENT WAVE."

How do you stop a skunk from smelling?
Stick two corks up its nose.

What did Noah say to his children about fishing from
the deck of the ark?
Go easy with the bait, kids. I've only got two
worms.

What is the best way to avoid diseases spread by
biting insects?
Don't bite any.

What is worse than finding a maggot in your apple?
Finding half a maggot in
your apple.

What do you get if you sit
under a cow?
A pat on the head.

Two flies were buzzing around looking for a snack
when they discovered a huge pile of dog poo. They
flew down and started tucking in. Suddenly one fly
let rip with an enormous smelly fart. The other fly
looked at him in disgust and said, "That's revolting.
Can't you see I'm trying to eat?"

CRAZY FOR POO

There is one beetle that loves poop so much it has been named after it. It is, of course, the dung beetle.

A male dung beetle gets a date by making a giant ball of dung which he rolls to his beloved. If the size of the dung ball impresses her, she climbs on top of it and the male rolls her away to an underground burrow to mate. She then lays her eggs in the dung ball and guards the precious pile of poop for up to 12 weeks. Meanwhile, the eggs inside develop into larvae. The larvae then tuck in to their delicious surroundings, eating their way out of the dung ball to begin their own poop-tastic lives dedicated to dung.

POOP PUZZLE

Here is a list of animals. Can you help busy Donald the dung beetle follow the trail to match each animal to the name of its poop? (Answers given at the bottom of the page.)

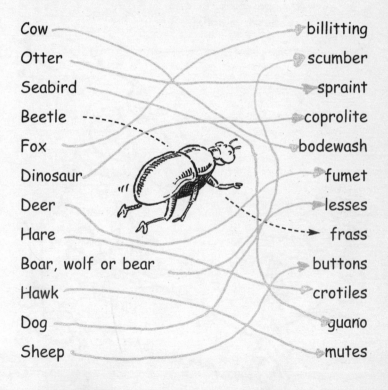

Cow	billitting
Otter	scumber
Seabird	spraint
Beetle	coprolite
Fox	bodewash
Dinosaur	fumet
Deer	lesses
Hare	frass
Boar, wolf or bear	buttons
Hawk	crotiles
Dog	guano
Sheep	mutes

MAD MYTH

TOP ANIMAL POOP FACTS

- Dragonfly larvae get about by ejecting water from their bums.

- Cats' urine glows under a black light.

- Winnie the Pooh was created by English author A.A. Milne in 1926.

- Rhinos stamp in their poop and then mark out their territory with their pooey footsteps.

- Hippos spread their scent by whirling their tails as they defecate.

- Bushbabies pee on their hands before travelling so they can follow the trail home again.

- Domestic dogs sometimes eat the poop from pet cats.

POOP!

TELL ME WHY

Q: Why does my faithful hound pee on my leg when I come home?

A: OK, so this doesn't happen to everyone, but I bet some of you know what I'm talking about! Yes, some dogs greet their owners by cocking their legs. Dogs in the wild often pee on their prey, their food and even each other as a mark of possession.

If your dog pees on your leg, don't despair. He or she is just being affectionate. In fact, your hound is so smitten that he wants to tell the whole doggy world that you belong to him! Doesn't that make you proud!

Does all this poop-tastic talk make your skin crawl? If not, the next chapter will. Turn the page to check out a world of bloodsucking, slithering, biting, disease-spreading parasites. Do you feel itchy yet?

CHAPTER SIX

ANIMAL PARASITES

An animal is a parasite if it lives in or upon another organism and draws its nutrition (food) directly from it. It has been estimated that 85 per cent of us are infected with parasites of one sort or another. They are everywhere. In fact, there are sure to be parasites within just 3m (10ft) of you right now!

So how do you know whether you are infested or a parasite-free zone? Next time you feel itchy, take a peek at this handy most-wanted list of parasites to find out where they live and what they can do!

BEDBUG

Found: In your bed, with thousands of its friends (that's one BIG slumber party!)
Profile: A flat, oval, red-brown insect 3–6mm ($\frac{1}{16}$ to $\frac{1}{8}$ in) in size

Bedbugs suck blood, injecting their victim with an anti-clotting agent, which means the blood stays runny — and yummy.

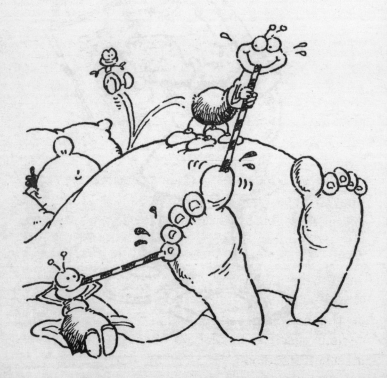

BLACK FLY

Found: Worldwide, especially Africa and Latin America
Profile: A small, fat, juicy fly up to 6mm ($1/8$ in) long

The male black fly likes nectar and the female sucks blood. Several kinds of black fly spread disease, including the very serious onchocerciasis, which can lead to blindness.

BLOOD FLUKE

Found: Worldwide
Profile: Type of parasitic flatworm

Young blood flukes hatch in rivers and lakes and turn into tadpole-like larvae called cercariae. Blood flukes hunt out a particular kind of water snail, so if you are wading or swimming in snail-infected water, beware — there may be blood flukes about. Blood flukes burrow into your skin and enter your bloodstream, finally settling in the veins in your gut. If you are in the tropics or the Far East then you could end up with a serious disease, leading to abscesses and severe internal bleeding.

About 200 million people worldwide suffer from diseases caused by blood flukes and without treatment they may die. Fortunately, however, there is a drug that kills blood flukes.

CHIGGER

Found: Worldwide
Profile: Between 0.1–16mm long and has three pairs of legs

The chigger is a type of mite that sucks up lymph (tissue fluid) and damaged skin cells, but hey — look on the bright side — at least it doesn't suck blood (*see* mite).

DADDY-LONG-LEGS (CRANE FLY)

Found: Worldwide
Profile: Bodies up to 2.5cm (1in) long with legs up to 3.8cm (1½in) long

Yes, amazingly, a daddy-long-legs is a blood-sucking parasite. It often swarms in late summer.

The larvae are called "leather jackets" (cool name). Why not tell your dad that you're going to give him a leather jacket for his birthday. He'll think you're the most generous person in the world — for a while, anyway!

FLEA

Found: Worldwide (even in the icy Arctic and Antarctic)
Profile: A tiny insect and the most famous of all the bloodsuckers. It is between 1–8mm long, with a flat shiny body

There are more than 1,800 varieties of flea. Although a flea has no wings, it can jump nearly 1m (3ft) into the air — that's the same as a human jumping more than 300m (980ft).

Relative to its size, a flea takes off with greater acceleration than the Space Shuttle and can leap up to 10,000 times in one hour!

Fleas are the real culprits (rather than the rats that the fleas lived on) responsible for spreading bubonic plague (Black Death) throughout Europe during the fourteenth century. The plague killed more than 50 per cent of the human population of Europe.

HOOKWORM

Found: Worldwide, especially tropical and subtropical countries
Profile: Between 7–11mm long. Any parasitic roundworm with hooked bits around its mouth

Hookworm larvae burrow into skin, often through the foot (which is why you must never walk barefoot in a hookworm-infested area). They travel through the bloodstream to the lungs then the gut. There, they grow into adult worms, latching on to the intestines where they suck blood, giving their victim anaemia, belly-ache and diarrhoea. More than 225 million people worldwide are infected with hookworm.

HORSEFLY

Found: Worldwide
Profile: A fly with short antennae. Can grow up to 2.5cm (1in) long

The males feed on nectar and the females are bloodsuckers. We call the British version a cleg-fly, and it can sneak up on you because it doesn't make a buzzing noise. The American model is called a greenhead because of its large green eyes. Horseflies can carry disease, such as anthrax, but usually you just get bitten and end up with a lump the size of a dinner plate.

KISSING BUG

Found: Worldwide
Profile: 1.5–2.5cm (^{1}/2–1in) long with a black body and yellow or red stripes

This bug comes out at night and no, you can't catch it from kissing. It often falls from trees or ceilings and feeds on exposed skin, frequently sucking the face (hence "kissing").

LEECH

Found: Ponds and lakes worldwide

There are 650 known species of leech, or blood-sucking worm of all sorts of sizes, colours and shapes. The leech attaches itself to a host with a sucking disk found at either end of its body, then it injects an anti-blood clotting agent and anaesthetic into the wound.

Leeches were used as a medical treatment for just about everything in the nineteenth century, when "bloodletting" was popular. Then they went out of favour and have only recently made a comeback in pioneering surgery, where they can perform a vital role of removing congested blood and preventing gangrene.

The anti-blood clotting and clot-digesting agents in leech saliva also make leeches useful for research into heart attacks and strokes. Scientists can now make several medical compounds from leech saliva and can "milk" a leech for its saliva without harming the leech itself.

TOP LEECH FACTS

- Leeches are related to earthworms.

- The largest leech ever recorded was 45cm (18in) long.

- A leech has 32 brains — that's 31 more than us!

- A leech will gorge itself until it's up to five times its initial body weight. Then it'll just fall off.

- Wales was once one of the major leech-collecting areas of Europe.

- A leech is not to be mistaken for the leechee (or lychee), a small oval fruit.

If you ever find a leech on your skin, it's important NOT to pull it off. If you do, the leech's mouthparts could be left in your skin and cause infection — and the risk of infection is more dangerous than the loss of blood. Victims should get out of the water, use an irritant (such as salt or heat) to make the leech let go and drop away, then treat the wound. The wound may bleed a bit because of the anticoagulant in leech saliva (*see above*).

LICE

Found: Worldwide
Profile: Tiny, at just 2–4mm (up to ⅛in) long

Lice have a natural lifespan of about 30 days and will die of starvation if kept off the body for more than 10 days

Head louse – lives in your hair. Lice lay their eggs near the surface of the scalp. White-coloured "nits" are left behind when the eggs hatch.

Body louse – lives and lays eggs in clothing; only visits skin to feed.

Crab louse – lives in body hair (all over – even eyebrows and eyelashes!).

Lice are killed by exposure to water hotter than 53.5°C (128°F) for more than five minutes, so to get rid of them, take a hot shower and (in the case of body lice) get some new clothes!

MAGGOT

Found: Wherever there are flies!
Profile: The larva of any species of fly up to 1.5cm (1/2in) long

Some maggots eat flesh but you can't blame the maggots — it's their parents, the flies, that choose to lay their eggs in living flesh. It's not all bad, though — blowfly maggots are sometimes used in surgery to clean up wounds and prevent gangrene.

MIDGE

Found: Common in sandy and northern areas, especially Scotland, Scandinavia and Canada
Profile: The smallest bloodsucking insect, at less than 1mm ($\frac{1}{32}$in) long

You often see midges in swarms in early spring and late autumn, especially at dusk and near water. They are especially annoying when you're trying to cook a barbecue in the evening.

MITE

Found: Worldwide
Profile: Tiny oval-bodied beastie with eight legs

The mite is a close relative of the tick, but much smaller, and just as gross. Many mites live in soil and help to rot and recycle vegetation.

Follicle mites live in your hair follicles and feed on skin oils.

173

House dust mites live in your carpets and there are at least two million in your bed, where they eat dead skin.

Itch mites burrow into your skin in sensitive areas, such as your fingers, wrists, elbows, belly button and private parts, and lay lots of eggs. Itch mites are itchy but harmless, although some people are allergic to their droppings. (*See also* Chigger.)

MOSQUITO

Found: Worldwide, including the Arctic
Profile: Small narrow body (up to 5mm long) with long slender wings and scales

There are more than 3,000 different mozzy species worldwide and they don't all live in hot places. Only the female mosquito gets its kicks from sucking blood. The male likes to stay at home and feed on nectar and water.

Mosquito-carried diseases include yellow fever, dengue fever, malaria and encephalitis. The *Anopheles* mosquito, which carries malaria, is estimated to have been responsible for half of all human deaths (apart from war and accidents) since the Stone Age.

ROBBER FLY

Found: In the air! Worldwide
Profile: Between 5–30mm long. Stout body covered with grey and yellow hairs and a bristly beard

This disgusting little creature ambushes you in midair, injects a nerve toxin into your body and then sucks out your insides. Fortunately humans are just too big to have their insides sucked out, so it's only creatures such as wasps, bees and dragonflies that need to beware!

TAPEWORM

Found: In the intestines of all animals with backbones and sometimes humans
Profile: Flat nematode (parasitic worm), from 1.3cm ($\frac{1}{2}$in) to 9m (30ft) long

The tapeworm uses hooks on its head to attach itself to the lining of its victim's intestines. It has no mouth or digestive canal, so it absorbs partially digested food through the surface of its body. Symptoms of infestation include diarrhoea, weight loss, general weakness, fatigue, shortness of breath and pain in the upper abdomen.

TICK

Found: Worldwide
Profile: Small round body. Size increases with eating, with eight legs

There are about 850 species of tick in the world. Most (called "hard ticks") have a hard shell and can endure extremes of cold. About 175 are called "soft ticks" and prefer drier conditions.

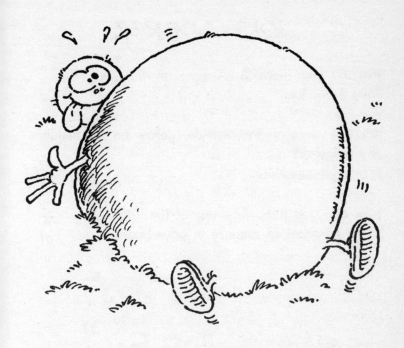

A tick attaches itself to a host by cutting a hole in the host's skin then literally gluing itself in place. The tick then sucks its host's blood for several days until it becomes so engorged that it falls off. A tick can increase its size by up to 150 times when it has fed — the biggest, bloated tick ever recorded was 2.8cm (1in) long.

Ticks carry loads of diseases including rickettsia, Lyme disease, Q fever, endemic typhus, relapsing fever and babesiosis. A tick should be removed gently from the skin so as not to break off its mouthparts.

JOKE CORNER

How do fleas travel?
They itch-hike.

What is white on the outside, yellow on the inside and wriggles?
A maggot sandwich.

How can you keep flies out of the kitchen?
Keep a bucket of manure in your bedroom.

I think you'll agree that parasites are a nasty bunch of creatures. But if you want to meet some real slime balls, turn the page to check out the most gooey, gunky and squidgy animals in the world.

Chapter Seven
Slime!

How many slimy animals can you name? A few obvious ones spring to mind first, such as snails, slugs, worms, jellyfish, frogs, toads, reptiles, snakes and octopuses. Yeah, yeah, the same old stuff, you might think.

But I bet there is loads of really cool stuff you *didn't* know about some of them AND plenty of other slimy creatures you've never even heard of!

Turn over to find out more . . .

SLIME MOULD

Myxomycete (slime mould to you and me) is so extraordinary that scientists can't agree whether to class it as a plant or an animal. This stuff is real X-Files slime, which can actually transform itself into something else.

When feeding, the slime mould looks like a large, often orange, ball of snot, which slowly moves as it eats up bacteria, spores and other organic matter. In this protoplasm stage it can often be found under the bark of rotting logs or between layers of rotting leaves. However, when the food runs out, the slime mould changes, in just a few hours, into a fungal fruiting body full of spores.

Some types of slime mould may form extensive fruitings on living plants, even grass. In fact, in Dallas, Texas, United States, in 1973, a bright yellow pulsating blobby slime mould called *Fuligo septica* covered large areas of lawn and freaked out the residents, who thought that blob alien mutant bacteria were invading them from outer space!

MAD MYTH

WORMS

Yeah, right, everyone knows about earthworms and how they eat soil . . . boring! But check out these other lesser-known sticks of slime.

Bristleworm

Also known as the aquatic earthworm, the bristleworm is a relative of the earthworm. It reproduces by budding, or splitting in two, and surprise, surprise, it's got bristles. Basically, therefore, it's a hairy worm that can swim.

Tubeworm

This amazing worm lives down on the floor of the Pacific Ocean near hydrothermal vents, where superheated water spurts out of the Earth's crust. A tubeworm can grow up to 3m (10ft) long and, get this, it doesn't have a mouth, eyes, stomach or bottom. Instead, it relies on bacteria inside its body turning the chemicals that spew out of the vents into food. "Ah, but how do the bacteria get into the worm in the first place" you ask? Well, it seems that the worm *does* have a mouth when it is younger but loses it as it grows. What a careless worm!

Horsehair worm

Also known as the Gordian worm, the horsehair worm can be found floating near the surface of calm water in the summer. Lots of these worms together resemble a tangled mass of horsehair.

Tubiflex worm

Also known as a sludge worm, the tubiflex worm spends its life with its head stuck in the mud at the bottom of ponds sucking up sludge with its tail waving out of the water. (This sucker clearly doesn't get out enough.)

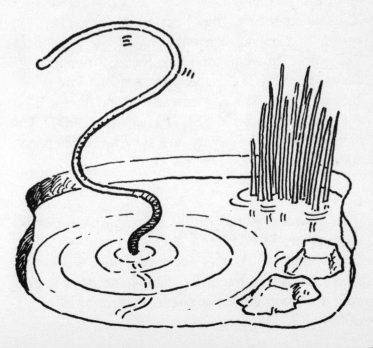

Pompeii worm

Another creature that lives near deep-sea vents, this animal currently holds the record for being able to withstand the highest temperatures, beating the Sahara desert ant into second place. The ant can withstand temperatures of up to 55°C (131°F), which is HOT! The Pompeii worm, however, can survive in temperatures up to 80°C (176°F).

Silkworm

The silkworm is not really a worm at all, but a caterpillar. It has been domesticated and used by humans for its silk for more than 4,000 years. It works hard! In just three days it can spin a cocoon out of a single thread of silk 600m (1,968ft) long.

Q: Why do earthworms come out to play after it rains?

A: You might think that earthworms appear after it rains because their little burrows get flooded, but you'd be wrong.

An earthworm's biggest problem in life, apart from being long and slimy, is that it can dry out very easily. So the real reason earthworms come out after a downpour is that they know there is no chance of dehydrating when the ground is so wet. Worms breathe through their skin and their skin needs to stay moist to work properly (just like a pair of lungs).

Also, this is the ideal time to do a spot of mating. Worms are hermaphrodites (they have both female and male sex organs), which means that although an earthworm is usually a sociable little soul, it can mate with itself when other worms are a bit thin on the ground (or under it). Anyway, mating is usually a very messy business if two worms are involved because they like to cover themselves in a big tube of snot.

MAD MYTH

To cure yourself of worms, eat horse-hairs chopped finely between two slices of bread and butter.

JOKE CORNER

What do you give an elephant with diarrhoea?
Plenty of space.

"Help, a shark has just bitten off my leg."
"Which one?"
"I don't know, they all look the same!"

Why do giraffes have long necks?
Because their feet smell.

What should you do with a white elephant?
Hold its nose until it turns grey.

HAGFISH

Hagfish are long, thin, pinkish eel-like fish with three hearts, no jaws, no stomach and one nostril. Not much going for them then, except maybe their amazing ability to produce large quantities of SLIME . . .

A hagfish uses this slime either to escape from predators or to trap its own prey. It's a real ocean vulture, feeding on dead and dying fish that have sunk to the bottom of the ocean. It uses a weird alien-looking probe with two pairs of rasps to burrow into its victim's flesh. Then it sucks out its insides, leaving just a sack of skin and bones.

Many fishermen have cut open fish they've caught only to find that they have no flesh. Instead, there's a bloated hagfish staring up at them.

A hagfish has such a slow metabolism that it can go up to seven months without eating. It can also tie a knot in itself and then move this knot down its body to remove any excess slime. If it gets slime up its one nostril, it just gives a powerful sneeze.

Hagfish are really primitive animals. They are some of the world's most ancient vertebrates (animals with backbones) and haven't changed much in the 300 million years or so since they left the evolutionary branch of backbony things that went on to develop into humans! Yes, we humans were hagfish, once upon a time . . . kind of humbling, isn't it?

JELLYFISH

Jellyfish are even more ancient than hagfish and have lived on Earth for more than 650 million years — that's even before the dinosaurs.

Jellyfish are found in all the world's oceans. There are about 200 known species and, of these, around 100 are harmful to humans.

The most famous is the Portuguese man-of-war with its transparent blue bladder and tentacles up to 30m (98ft) long, found in the seas off the southeast USA and the Caribbean. The most deadly, however, is the Australian box jellyfish (*see Animal killers, pages 59–60*).

Jellyfish get around by a kind of jet propulsion, shooting water out of their bells. One type of Mediterranean jellyfish is just 3cm (1in) in diameter yet it can travel up to 1,100m (3,600ft) a day — that's the same as a 1.8m (6ft) human swimming more than 50km (31m).

Oh, yes, and they're 95 per cent water. They have no heart, no brain, and no blood, yet they manage to keep upright in the water because of special balance sacs similar to those humans have in their ears!

SNAILS

A snail is basically a slimy mollusc related to oysters, clams and other shellfish. The posh name for its shell is *Helix aspersa*.

Snails produce a slimy mucus that immediately hardens upon contact with the air to form a tough protective surface for them to cruise around on. Because of this, a snail can even creep along the edge of a razor blade without getting injured! A snail moves around on a flat "foot" underneath its body. The muscles in the foot contract and expand to create a rippling motion.

Some snails can grow over 30cm (12in) long. The largest snail ever recorded was called Gee Geronimo, a giant African snail found in Sierra Leone in 1976. It weighed in at a staggering 1kg (2lb) and measured nearly 40cm (16in) from nose to tail.

Q: Why should you politely refuse if an armadillo offers you his hanky?

A: Because armadillos are the only other animals, apart from humans and a couple of monkeys, that carry leprosy – and snot is an effective form of transmission. OK, it's only about 5 per cent of armadillos of the nine-banded variety that have the disease and it's not that easy to catch, so there's no need to give away your pet 'dillo just yet. However, it's best to scarper if he starts flicking bogeys at you.

TELL ME WHY

AMOEBA

An amoeba is a one-celled blob of slime (called protoplasm) with a stretchy cell wall and a nucleus. It is typically about 0.0025mm (0.000985in) in size.

An amoeba moves by pushing out a part of itself into a false foot and then "streaming" into this part. When it feeds on smaller organisms, the amoeba sends out pairs of false feet which surround the organism, creating a hole, or vacuole. Acid is pumped into the vacuole to digest the food and then the waste is expelled through the outer layer of the cell. It reproduces by simply splitting in two.

Now you've read about slime, why not check out the final chapter to see how humans match up in the grossology league table.

CHAPTER EIGHT

HUMANS - THE GROSSEST ANIMALS OF THEM ALL

"Mirror mirror on the wall, who is the grossest of them all?"

Well, have you looked at yourself recently? We humans have got fairly gross bodies. We're full of germs and bacteria and saliva, snot and slime. Read on to find out about these AND our horrible habits, so gross they're in a separate category of their own (see page 207).

BUSY BACTERIA

Did you know that you've got about 100 million bacteria in your mouth and you're swallowing millions right now! In fact your mouth is a jungle. There are more than 100 different species of bacteria living in it. Some bacteria like to live on your teeth. Others prefer your gums, the roof of your mouth or the cracks in your tongue.

There are also hundreds of species of fungi, viruses and single-celled organisms in your mouth and hundreds of microscopic creatures that haven't even been identified yet. The good news is that this disgusting menagerie is good for us. It actually forms a balanced ecosystem in the mouth of a healthy individual.

Scientists have also measured that the skin of your armpits is home to as many as three million bacteria per sq cm (half a million per sq in). Even places like your forearms have about 84,000 bacteria per sq cm (13,000 per sq in).

If you were to remove all the moisture from your body, then a tenth of your "dry weight" would be bacteria.

SWEATY FEET

You've got about two million sweat glands, and about an eighth of those are in your feet.

GUT ROT

There are 400 types of germs in your colon alone, and they account for about 1.5kg (3lb) of your body weight! And there are BILLIONS of germs in your guts. These germs produce gas, which is why you fart.

SLIMEBALL

And you know the stuff that makes your urine yellow? That's called urea. Well, it's in your mouth, too, and your sweat — and that means it's all over your clothes because you sweat all over your body.

Yeuuch! Basically you're slimier than a slug! You produce about 2l (3pt) of saliva each day, and your guts produce about 2l (3pt) of snot each day, too.

WAXWORK

Also, you've got 2,000 glands in your ears just to produce ear wax.

SHEDDING SKIN

And if you think that reptiles are gross when they shed their skin, YOU do it all the time. The top layers of your skin are dead and are continually coming off. In fact, you lose about 36 million cells every day — that's 13 billion a year. (Sad to think that we spend millions each year on beauty products and then rub it on skin that is actually dead!)

MAD MYTH

If you dream of fish, someone you know is expecting a baby.

HOW GROSS
CAN YOU GO?

So you think you're not as gross as a frigate
bird or a hagfish. Why not try this quiz? You'll
be surprised to find you're MUCH grosser than
you thought.

1. **You're sitting on a crowded bus and you
suddenly get the urge to pick
your nose. What do you
do?**

a) Wait until you get
home.

b) Produce a large
tissue and blow
your nose quietly.

c) Wait until no
one is watching
and have a quick
pick, pretending
to scratch your
nose.

d) Have a deep troll,
grunting noisily with
satisfaction and wipe a big
loogie on the coat of the person in front.

2. You've been playing football after school and you're hot and sweaty. You'll be late home if you take a shower. What do you do?

a) Leave 15 minutes early giving you lots of time to shower before you go home.

b) Race home and have a shower when you get back.

c) Wet your hair and fake it — no one will ever know.

d) Go home and hang your sweaty shirt on a radiator so you can wear it for the rest of the week.

3. How often do you cut your toenails?

a) Every week.

b) Once a month.

c) You wait until your nails are growing into your toes and it's getting painful to walk.

d) Never: they should break off naturally when they are ready (besides, you're growing toe jam).

4. You're babysitting and you find your kid sister cleaning the toilet with your dad's toothbrush. What do you do?

a) Grass up your sister when your dad gets home.

b) Give the brush a good wash then put it back in its place.

c) Shake the brush a bit then put it back in its place.

d) Put the brush back and go and watch TV.

5. How long is your tongue?
a) Pathetically short.
b) I can touch my nose.
c) I can lick my eyebrows.
d) I can close the door without getting out of bed.

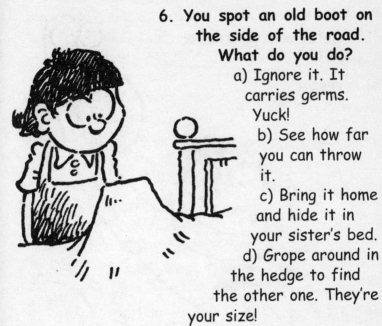

6. You spot an old boot on the side of the road. What do you do?
   a) Ignore it. It carries germs. Yuck!
   b) See how far you can throw it.
   c) Bring it home and hide it in your sister's bed.
   d) Grope around in the hedge to find the other one. They're your size!

7. How often do you clean your teeth?
a) After every meal.
b) Whenever you remember.
c) When they get rough and sticky.
d) Never: chewing loogies is the best way to prevent cavities.

8. What's your ideal pet?
a) A fluffy wuffy kitten or puppy.
b) A reptile.

c) An Ecuador tree frog. Animals that can disguise themselves as lumps of poo are so cool.
d) Bacteria.

Add up your score, giving yourself 0 points for every (a) answer, 3 points for every (b) answer, 5 points for (c), and 10 points for (d). Turn to page 237 for the results.

GROSS HABITS

We must be the only animals to have developed gross habits because we enjoy them. You could fill a whole book with the history of gross human habits, but let's just take a look at a couple — nose-picking and fart-loving. (I say fart-loving rather than just farting because while most animals fart, we're the only ones that take a positive delight in it!)

MAD MYTH

Put mucous from a dog's eye in your own and you'll be able to see ghosts.

NOSE-PICKING

Nobody knows when humankind dragged itself out of prehistory and discovered nose-picking. Like the discovery of fire, it was undoubtedly a special moment. Of course, in reality, it probably started when we evolved fingers and nostrils.

SNOTTY STUDY

We all know someone who is a champion rooter. Maybe it's your mum or dad, your older brother, or even your granny having a quick pick behind her hanky. OK, it's disgusting, but people still do it and some scientists did a study recently that actually proves it. They published their research in the *Journal of Psychiatry* in February 1995. However, they don't call it nose-picking, rooting, caving or loogie-mining. They call it rhinotillexo-mania (rhino = nose, tillexis = habit of picking at something, mania = obsession). So, just think, your granny could be a rhinotillexomaniac!

HAND-PICKED

The researchers sent their "Rhinotillexomania Questionnaire" to 1,000 residents picked (!) at random in Dane County, Wisconsin, United States. It asked them to answer several questions on nose-picking, which it defined as the:

"Insertion of a finger (or other object) into the nose with the intention of removing dried nasal secretions."

The results are very illuminating.

Of the 1,000 questionnaires sent out, 254 surveys were completed and returned.

- 8.7 per cent reckon they have never picked their nose. (I doubt that. Everybody has had a good root at some time in their life.)

- 91 per cent said they had picked and were still at it. Yet only half of those questioned thought that nose-picking was common.

- 9.2 per cent classed their rooting as "more than average".

- 25.6 per cent dug daily, 22.3 per cent did it up to five times a day, and three people owned up to doing it at least every hour.

- 55.5 per cent spent 1–5 minutes at it, 23.5 per cent spent 5–15 minutes, and 0.8 per cent (2 people) spent 15–30 minutes a day picking their noses. One person actually claimed his caving went on for more than two hours a day.

- 18 per cent said their nose-picking caused nose bleeds, and two people reported perforation of the nasal septum.

CAVING TOOLS

- 65.1 per cent favoured their index finger, 20.2 per cent their little finger, and 16.4 per cent their thumb as their chosen caving tool.

- 90.3 per cent disposed of the boogers in a tissue or a handkerchief, 28.6 per cent used the floor, 7.6 per cent wiped it on furniture, and 8 per cent ate it (the most eco-friendly solution).

So, what can we deduce from this invaluable research? Well, it's clear that rooting is very common. So next time your granny disappears behind the sofa and starts making little grunting sounds, you can guess what she's up to. And if your dad starts growing the fingernails on one of his hands because he claims he is "learning the guitar" be very suspicious!

Of course, we don't know how many surveys *weren't* returned by extreme rhinotillexomaniacs who just couldn't spare the time (or a free hand) so it could be even more widespread than we think!

TELL ME WHY

Q: How much snot does a healthy person produce each day?

A: About 1.4l (⅓g). Yes, you make it and then you swallow it.

TELL ME WHY

FAKE SNOT RECIPE

- Make a borax solution by putting $\frac{1}{8}$ cup of borax laundry booster into a litre ($\frac{1}{2}$ pt) of warm water and shaking well until the borax dissolves. Allow the mixture to cool.

- Put 2 spoonfuls of Elmer's glue into a cup and add 3 spoonfuls of water.

- Stir in 3 drops of green food dye.

- Pour into a plastic bag and add 1 spoonful of the borax solution. Rub the sides of the bag together to mix.

Result — a bag of fake snot to fool your friends!

(Just to prove how gross we all are, how many of you are actually going to make this snot recipe?)

JOKE CORNER

What goes peck, peck, peck, boom?
A chicken in a minefield.

What did the fly say after he hit the windscreen?
I'd do it again if only I had the guts.

How do you tell when a moth farts?
It flies in a straight line.

What happens when a bomb goes off in the middle of a herd of cows?
Udder destruction.

What do frogs order in restaurants?
French Flies!

Where do you find a dog with no legs?
Just where you left it.

Why do ducks have flat feet?
To stamp out forest fires.

Why do elephants have flat feet?
To stamp out ducks.

A little story . . .
A hyena and a turtle are having a drink at a
watering hole when an elephant arrives.
The elephant stares for a moment then lifts up his
enormous foot and squashes the little turtle flat.
"What did you do that for?" asked the hyena.
"Well," replied the elephant, "about eighty years ago
that turtle bit my foot. Finally I found
the little sucker and got my revenge."
"But how can you be sure it was that turtle that bit
you after such a long time?" asked the hyena.
With a modest smile the elephant replied, "Oh, I
have turtle recall."

Another little story . . .

DUNG'S TOP 10 GROSS FACTS ABOUT US

1. Right-handed people sweat more on their left arm and left-handed people sweat more on their right arm.

2. We have stuff that collects in the corners of our eyes when we're asleep. Sleeping dust, eye gunk, eye jam — it has no scientific name.

3. A lump of poop is roughly 50 per cent bacteria.

4. It takes about 24 hours for food to pass from our plates into our mouths and then out of our bottoms.

5. The yellow gloopy thing that comes out of a popped blackhead is dried-up grease from our sebaceous glands.

6. If we scooped up all the bacteria from our intestines it would fill a jam jar.

7. It takes less than 10 seconds for a piece of swallowed food to reach our stomachs.

8. Our small intestine is larger than our large intestine. It's called small because it's narrow.

9. The germs in our faeces can pass through up to 10 layers of toilet paper.

10. We smell best when we're about 10 years old. From then on, our sense of smell starts to decline.

FARTING

What about farting? Don't pretend that you never do it: scientists reckon that an average healthy person farts about 16 times a day. (Now that's a scary statistic on those days when you manage to let rip your entire daily allowance of air biscuits before you've even had your breakfast!)

We've already seen that lots of animals can do impressive things with their guffs, but we turn bombers into an art form. Take Joseph Pujol, for example.

MAD MYTH

To dream of a lizard means you have a secret enemy.

HALL OF FAME
Joseph Pujol — "Le Fartiste"

Joseph Pujol was born in Marseilles, France, on 1 June 1857.

While in the army, he used to entertain his friends with his amazing ability to fart at will. He could suck up air and blow it out again. He could even do the same trick with water. He renamed himself "Le Petomane" (meaning "The Fartiste").

After his "success" in the army, Pujol returned to Marseilles and became a professional. His notoriety spread and soon folks came from all over Marseilles to see him perform. Then, in 1892, he was signed up at Paris's most famous nightspot, the Moulin Rouge. Soon, everyone in Paris was talking about him and he quickly became one of the most celebrated and richest performers of his time.

Pujol would dress up in a formal coat, red trousers, gloves and shiny leather shoes. He would then spend the evening performing lots of incredible farting tricks and impressions. He would send a jet of water 5m (16ft) out of his behind, and even play the trombone from his

backside! His audiences found him so hilarious that nurses were on hand every night to help those people who fainted with laughter.

His success lasted until about 1900 when the public gradually lost interest. When he finally retired, he moved to Toulon with his family, where he founded and ran a biscuit factory and happily lived out the rest of his days. After his death in 1945, doctors offered his loving family 25,000 francs for permission to examine his corpse. His family declined.

GROSS AND GREEDY

Finally, we are greedy with a capital G. That's not just food. It's the entire world's resources.

As Gandhi once famously said, "The Earth has enough for every man's need, but not enough for every man's greed."

We are damaging and destroying many of the world's natural resources because of the greed of the richest nations. The United States, for example, has 6 per cent of the world's population but uses 30 per cent of the world's energy resources.

Every person in the United Kingdom uses, on average, 20 times more resources than every person in developing nations; and in developing nations, 36,000 young children die every day (that's one child every 2.4 seconds) because of poverty.

On average, people in the West eat 30—40 per cent more calories than they need while 800 million people elsewhere in the world don't have enough food.

We spend millions each year on slimming products then pretend there is a world shortage of food. Yet the world already produces enough grain alone to give everyone 2,500 calories per day. (We just like to hoard it for ourselves.)

STUFF AND NONSENSE

And we love hoarding. Our need for STUFF is so great that we chop down rainforests and pollute the environment in our quest for more. Yet one of the fastest-growing industries is self-storage because people don't have enough room to store their essential must-have stuff!

WHAT A WASTE!

What about the stuff we throw away? Each household in the United Kingdom throws away about one ton (tonne) of rubbish each year — that's a total of 20 million tons (tonnes). The United States produces about 5.5 billion tons (tonnes) of waste each year, including 8 million TV sets and 2.5 million bottles an *hour*. About 200 billion cans, bottles, plastic cartons and paper cups are thrown away each year in the developed world.

If that wasn't enough, we cause death and suffering to millions of animals, too. Every year, more than 1,000 animals and plants disappear from the Earth for ever because of our greed for more land for building and farming.

What a downer! So, if you've loved reading about the animals in this book, remember that we are truly the grossest animals of them all!

Did you think it was going to be a happy ending . . . ?

OK, turn over for a last bit of light relief.

JOKE CORNER

How do hens talk to each other?
They use fowl language.

What do you get when you cross a mink with a
kangaroo?
A fur coat with pockets.

What is yellow and smells of bamboo?
Panda puke.

Why do dogs scratch themselves?
Because they're the only ones who know where it
itches.

What did one frog in the bog say to the other frog in the bog?
Time's sure fun when you're having flies!

What has five feet, three eyes and two tails?
A horse with spare parts.

ABBREVIATIONS USED IN THIS BOOK

Metric:
mm = millimetre(s)
cm = centimetre(s)
m = metre(s)
km = kilometre(s)
km/h = kilometres per hour
ml = millilitre(s)
l = litre(s)
g = gram(s)
kg = kilogram(s)
°C = degrees Celsius

Imperial:
in = inch(es)
m = mile(s)
mph = miles per hour
fl oz = fluid ounce(s)
g = gallon(s)
lb = pound(s)
st = stone(s)
°F = degrees Fahrenheit

Gross Glossary

Bacteria   Microscopic single-celled organisms. They are usually spherical, long and thin or spiral-shaped. Many can be killed with anti-biotics, but are actually very important for life.

Barf   A really cool word for being sick. It is onomatopoeic, which means that it sounds like the thing it is describing — like *cuckoo* and *sizzle*. If a crowd of people can't stop being sick then they're taking part in a "barforama".

Blood bank   A place where blood and blood products for transfusion are stored. The first recorded blood transfusion took place in 1666 when a British physician, Richard Lower transferred blood between two animals with terrible results. It wasn't until 1901 that doctors began to understand how to transfer blood safely between humans. But the first blood bank wasn't set up until the late 1930s.

Bogey   A piece of nasal mucus. Also a score of one above par in golf!

Burp   The air that escapes from your stomach and comes out of your mouth.

Carrion   Dead and rotting flesh.

Coprolite   Fossilized dinosaur poop.

Deep troll   Rooting using the elbow and shoulder for maximum leverage. (*See* Rooting)

Defecate   Grown-up word for pooping.

Dung   Animal poo and the title of this book! The word *dungaree* which we think of today as a type of overall, is actually a kind of fabric. A few hundred years ago, certain fabrics were dipped in a bath full of dung as part of the dying process. Dungaree was manufactured like this — hence the name — *Poohee*!

Dust grolley   A horrible mixture of dust, hair and biscuit crumbs that blocks up vacuum cleaners.

Exoskeleton   Some animals, especially insects, have this rigid body shell which gives support and protection.

Faeces   Grown-up word for poop.

Fart   We swallow lots of gas all the time, and when we digest our food, the bacteria in our gut produce many different gases, including carbon dioxide, methane, nitrogen and even hydrogen. The more sulphur there is in your diet, the smellier your farts. Hydrogen sulphide is the gas that makes farts smelly. Food like cauliflower, eggs and meat create smelly farts because of their high sulphur content. Top farting expressions include: air-biscuit, dropping a chalupa, guff, letting rip, bottom-burping, cutting the cheese, carpet-creeper, squeaker, trump, back-draft, flurpy, low-flying geese, busting a grumpy, peaches, crunchy frog.

Fartiste   A person who makes a living out of busting a grumpy in front of an audience.

Fecologist   Someone who studies poop.

Flatulence   Excess air in your stomach or intestines which usually results in lots of farts and burps.

Frass   The name given to the faeces of the larvae of any insect. So caterpillars and maggots alike poop frass.

Germ Any microbe that causes disease. Doctors only started believing in the existence of germs during the late nineteenth century. Before the introduction of antiseptic, doctors and surgeons actually spread more disease than they cured because they didn't even wash their hands or instruments between patients.

Glob A mass or lump of semi-liquid consistency, e.g. mud, mucus.

Globule A small globe or round drop of liquid.

Gob A mouth or a mouthful of something slimy. To spit.

Grossology This is the study of all things gross. So animal grossology is the study of gross animal behaviour.

Guatemalan dorito frog A small orange-brown amphibian from Central America. It camouflages itself as a popular potato snack to avoid being eaten. Unfortunately this particular disguise has had exactly the opposite effect, and quickly led to the extinction of the species!

Hawking Clearing your throat noisily.

Hurl To be sick. Hurling is also a sport — but it is more like hockey than hocking!

Incontinent   Unable to control movements of the bladder or bowels or both.

Metabolism   All the chemical processes that take place inside a living organism in order to create energy.

Microbe   A tiny living organism, especially bacteria and viruses.

Nasal septum   The cartilage that separates your nostrils.

Parasite   Any animal that lives in or upon another organism and draws its nutrition (food) directly from it. If you're always begging food from your friends, then you're a parasite.

Phlegm   A thick goo that is produced in your lungs and may come out when you cough. However, if a person is described as phlegmatic, it doesn't mean they can't stop coughing. It means they are very calm and unemotional.

Piles   Also known as haemorrhoids, which are swollen veins in your bottom. They can be very painful and itchy. Not a subject to bring up at the dinner table.

Poop   Who would have thought such a little word could have so many meanings? Originally it meant to cheat someone and the stern of a ship or a short blast made in a hollow tube. Finally it came to mean poo.

Pooper scooper   A device for cleaning up after a pet. This could be anything from a plastic bag to a dumper truck, depending whether you have a Yorkshire Terrier or an African elephant.

Protoplasm   The material that makes up the living part of a cell.

Puke   In medieval times people used to make expensive clothes out of puke. No, really! It's a posh kind of woollen cloth. Later, the word puke came to mean a blueish black coloured die (puke is this season's grey, darling!). Finally it came to mean sick. Shakespeare uses the word 'puking' in his play *As You Like It*.

Retch   To try to vomit without results! Here's a handy tip if you want to stop retching: start vomiting.

Rhinotillexomaniac   Someone who just can't stop picking their nose. Does that describe anyone you know?

Rooting   A particularly obsessive form of loogie-mining in which the rooter inserts a large part of a chosen finger and rotates for several minutes. Also known as caving.

Toxic   The Greek word for bow (as in *bow and arrow*) was *toxon* and toxikon meant 'of the bow' — referring to the poison that they used on their arrows. Today it refers to anything poisonous.

Virus   The smallest and simplest microbes. They can't even be seen with a microscope. They can only grow inside another living cell and they cannot be killed with antibiotics.

Vomit   To eject stuff from the stomach through the mouth. If the stuff isn't from your stomach or it doesn't come out of your mouth, then it isn't really proper vomiting. OK, if you put your hand over your mouth and it squirts out of your nose, that counts too. But ears definitely don't qualify!

iNDEX

"How gross can you go?" quiz results

0 You're a real no-hoper. You've never done anything gross in your life. For you, "eating your greens" means tucking into a plate of healthy vegetables.

1–40 You can be dull but have occasional flashes of gross brilliance.

41–69 With a little more practice you'll be loogie-mining on the bus with the pros. Go on! Surrender to your baser instincts!

70–100 You have no friends and a natural talent for ignoring both personal and public sanitation. You are a truly revolting individual. Well done!